MOON SPELLS

Journal

Guided Rituals, Reflections, and Meditations

DIANE AHLQUIST
Author of *Moon Spells*

Adams Media
New York   London   Toronto   Sydney   New Delhi

Adams Media
An Imprint of Simon & Schuster, Inc.
57 Littlefield Street
Avon, Massachusetts 02322

First Adams Media trade paperback edition June 2020

ADAMS MEDIA and colophon are trademarks of Simon & Schuster.

For information about special discounts for bulk purchases, please contact Simon & Schuster Special Sales at 1-866-506-1949 or business@simonandschuster.com.

The Simon & Schuster Speakers Bureau can bring authors to your live event. For more information or to book an event contact the Simon & Schuster Speakers Bureau at 1-866-248-3049 or visit our website at www.simonspeakers.com.

Interior design by Julia Jacintho
Interior images © 123RF/jaysi

Manufactured in the United States of America

3 2021

ISBN 978-1-5072-1366-7
ISBN 978-1-5072-1367-4 (ebook)

DEDICATION

I dedicate this book to those who seek self-realization. These people are my readers, who hail from all different parts of the globe. They may walk a different road, but they keep walking! They discover new things and find compassion for themselves, each other, and the planet.

ACKNOWLEDGMENTS

With deep appreciation, I want to thank my family and extended family for all of their continued support. I also want to express my gratitude to all of my editors at Simon & Schuster.

A shout of appreciation to some special guys: Chris Duffy, just because I like him; Bob Irwin, who is always distinguished and accommodating; David Stahl, for making our meals; Chris Sake; Daniel; Joshua; Ethen; and Johnny. Thanks to my husband, Adrian, who still thinks a pendulum is only something on a grandfather clock. Really, Adrian?

Thanks as well to the ladies in my life: my sister Marie; Lori; Janet Osterholt; Christine Soderbeck; Olivia; Deanna Fritz; and the list goes on. A special acknowledgment to Shelly Hagen and Dee for their contribution to this journal. Those who helped me with research are much appreciated. Robin Bergevin, my assistant, gives me time to breathe. Thanks, mother, for your kolacky recipe on my website. (Yes, that's Czech.) All the best to Lesley Melahn and her horse Brad Pitt (don't ask—I didn't name him) for helping me gallop faster to make changes to my present situation.

I know I tend to thank a lot of people, but it's all about gratitude. I thank you! Blessings.

CONTENTS

INTRODUCTION

As the closest, largest, and brightest object illuminating the radiant darkness of our night sky, it's no wonder that the moon holds a mystical place in our human consciousness. The cosmic dance between the earth, the sun, and the moon is a ritual as powerful and timeless as the universe. Life on Earth as we know it would not exist without our solar and lunar relationships. These interactions shape and continually influence the development and sustainability of life each day.

Acting as a stabilizing and moderating force, the moon's gravitational pull makes the climate on Earth habitable, the seasons predictable, temperatures tolerable, and winds temperate. Additionally, this magnetic attraction powers the tides. The constant rhythm of lunar illumination of the new, waxing, full, and waning phases signals critical reproductive cycles for many animal species. When I look up at the moon at night, I am reminded of our intimate relationship to the vast, mysterious cosmos and all that is unknown. The moon is a portal between worlds: It is a spiritual intermediary between the dark yet to be known and the already illuminated familiar.

When you choose to be mindful of the moon's influence, attune to its rhythms, and partner yourself with lunar strength and potency, you can harness its powerful, supportive, and transformative energy. Tapping in to this energy connects you with larger cosmic forces that will empower you and impact your life in ways you can only imagine.

Whether you have already realized the moon's effects on you or you are nurturing a new relationship with the moon, keeping track of your feelings and actions in *Moon Spells Journal* will be very illuminating. Journaling, engaging in fun activities, and conducting rituals related to the moon are easy and effective ways to become attentive to, cultivate a connection with, and harness the power of the lunar cycle to help you shape your life. In *Moon Spells Journal*, I've given you prompts for each moon phase in each month in order to fuel your alignment with the magic of the moon.

For example, a waxing moon's energetic momentum increases on its journey to becoming full. In this phase, you will look to increase or invite things into your life, with rituals and spells such as Attract $100 Into Your Life or Practice Candle Magic to Attract Love. By contrast, the waning moon phase is a time to decrease, release, and eliminate whatever it is your body, mind, and spirit need to get rid of. That's why you'll find exercises like Release Self-Doubt or Let Bad Habits Sail Away in this phase.

While tracking the impact of each moon phase in your life, you will begin to notice patterns in physical, emotional, mental, and spiritual aspects of your being. These will empower you with knowledge that can improve your ability to set goals, make decisions, and plan the timing of key activities in your life (such as launching new endeavors or letting go of unproductive relationships). The unique way you attune to the moon will be deeply personal and reflective of your own consciousness, but this book may help you better:

• Connect with the ebb and flow of eternal and deep cosmic creative energies.
• Strengthen your natural instincts.
• Synchronize your body cycles for enhanced energy, health, and well-being.
• Intensify your relationship with yourself, which may help you better appreciate, understand, and take care of yourself.
• Supercharge your intentions.

Because every phase of the moon is a spectacular sight, as often as possible, take time to step outside into the night and soak in the fabulous expansiveness of the night sky and our beautiful cosmic dance partner. Listen to and rest in the harmony of the universe and then in your own being. Tune in to the fullness of your being in an open, wordless fashion. Feel the connection between the eternal universe and the essence of your being; resonate with the magnetism between the lunar and terrestrial; let the realization of the order and balance sink in and merge with and attune your energies to the great heavens or cosmos.

For us here on Earth, the moon represents the rhythm of light and dark; lunar and solar; seen and unseen; yin and yang; attraction and release. Paying attention to the rhythm of the moon infuses your life with its immense power. By consciously noting the phases of the moon and how the moon cycle process plays out in your life, you gain deeper understanding and insight into ancient creative power. You instinctively move to the lunar rhythm; your actions become inspired and informed by the stable yet ever-changing flow of moon wisdom; and your life is transformed through cosmic enlightenment.

HOW TO USE THIS BOOK

In order to make the most of *Moon Spells Journal*, it's important to understand the type of energy associated with each moon phase, and how to use that energy to your advantage. Certain lunar phases best coincide with setting certain intentions, following through with certain actions, and executing certain plans.

Let's start with learning how to set an intention. *Setting an intention* simply means identifying and focusing on a request and being very clear about your desired outcome. As the saying goes, "What you think about, you bring about," so the more specific you can be, the better. For example, you might start out thinking, "I want a new relationship." That's a pretty broad statement. Get down to the nitty gritty! What does your desired person look like? Is it important that this person be smart, funny, serious, or ambitious? Should this person enjoy things like hiking, live music, cooking, or animals? Do you want this person to be a certain age or work in a certain field? You can break down any kind of request in this same way. Write it all down so you can refer to it and remind yourself of your exact intention.

Depending on what your intention is, you'll want to focus on it (and any activities related to it) during the appropriate phase:

 **New Moon:** The phase when the moon is not visible to us. This signifies fresh starts, and it's a great time to contemplate the things you'd like to work on during the coming lunar cycle.

 **Waxing Moon:** When the moon is increasing in size in the sky, leading up to the full moon. During this phase, as the moon's power is intensifying, set intentions related to the things you want to increase or augment in your life. For example, now is an ideal time to focus on a raise or promotion.

Full Moon: The height of the moon's power! This is the time to seal your intention and trust that it will come to fruition.

Waning Moon: The moon begins to fade from view, becoming smaller each night. Set an intention now for things you want to release or decrease in your life, like a friendship that isn't working, painful emotions, or old beliefs that aren't serving you.

You'll find a lot of ideas and exercises in this book for coupling your intentions with the moon's energy. The waxing and waning moon sections include more prompts than the other sections because it is time of more action, one way or the other. Many entries have space for writing or drawing; if you need more space, simply grab a separate piece of paper. The goal is simply to work with the current phase of the moon and its associated power so you can bring everything you dream of into your life!

January

Find Your
True Path

As we usher in a new calendar year, this moon cycle is a soft, fluid period of early development when all is promising and full of potential. It's a quiet, introspective month meant for listening to inner thoughts, reflecting on and learning from past accomplishments and failures, and imagining a positive future. The gifts of this month's moon (and they are gifts) are best realized through the subtle energies of intuition rather than intellect.

Even as daylight increases and winter slowly progresses toward spring, often the moon's energy is sluggish and change appears slight, shadowy, and below the surface. But do not disdain the dark, cold, meagerness, or isolation of winter; instead, embrace and enjoy the solitude and break before the coming activity of spring.

During this month, conserve energy, spend some time in contemplation and meditation, relish memories, journal, forgive, and release. Concentrate on and pamper yourself. Explore your dreams and desires, nurture your well-being, and revive your health. Focus on your convictions and prepare to embark on the path that will allow you to enact what you want to see come to fruition in the coming year.

Get to Know Yourself Better

The beginning of the year is a great time to take stock and celebrate who you are! Check in with yourself to assess your likes, dislikes, skills, feelings, and goals. Ask yourself these questions:

1. When do I feel most at peace?

2. What makes me feel creative?

3. Is there anything I want to learn more about?

4. Do I need to refresh my current skills?

5. Do I feel supported by my current social network?

6. What inspires me to be a better person?

7. What causes me to feel most stressed?

8. Are there things in my life that are not serving me that I can let go of?

9. Where do I want to be in five years?

10. Who can I ask for advice or assistance?

Set Some Goals for the Year

New moon + new year = new ideas! This is the time to give thought to your wildest dreams and loftiest ambitions. As the old axiom asks, "What would you do if you knew you could not fail?" Nothing is off the table and everything is possible. Make a simple list of your goals for the upcoming year. Don't worry about how you will accomplish any of them just yet; just jot them down.

Give Your Idea Wings

There's no better time to send your ideas soaring than on the day or night of a new moon. The new moon is an energetic match for your new ideas—just as the moon is being born, so are your ideas. In the following space, draw two wings and write a realistic idea in the center (for example, *Get a job interview*). There is no right or wrong way to draw or design the wings; just make sure the wings touch your words.

 When you're done, look at your drawing and close your eyes. Visualize the wings carrying your idea off the page, going through the ceiling, to the sky, past the moon, and into the universe. Say some closing words, such as "And so it is."

◑ Reboot Your Goals That Didn't Work

Not every goal is going to work out, and it has nothing to do with your abilities—sometimes a goal just doesn't fit with your life, or you find, after an initial effort, that it's just not something you're really interested in after all. But a goal that doesn't work is just a goal that's ripe for morphing into another opportunity.

If your plans aren't panning out the way you envisioned, take the lesson from it and move on to something else. The waxing moon is a time for rebuilding, for taking the remnants of one dream and using them to establish a new one. This is what life is all about—evaluating, adapting, and moving forward! Think of a goal you set in the past but would like to change. Rearrange it into something that works for you now and write it here.

Old Goal ⟶ New Goal

Take a Mindful Walk in Nature

The waxing moon is time to collude with the power of Mother Nature and to draw from her strength. You'll find that it's easier to engage with the moon's phases when you are tuned in to the natural energies surrounding you. To practice this, take a mindful walk through nature, with no headphones, no talking, no distractions. Simply focus on the beauty around you and let it inspire your creativity and strength. As you walk, engage your senses and observe.

• What do you see? What colors is nature showing off where you are?

_____

_____

_____

_____

• What do you hear? Birds? Squirrels chattering? Airplanes overhead?

_____

_____

_____

_____

• Do you smell anything? Flowers, fresh-cut grass, smoke from a nearby bonfire?

_____

_____

_____

_____

_____

• What do you feel? Is the temperature hot, cold, temperate? Is it raining, snowing, humid?

_____

_____

_____

_____

Try to make mindfulness exercises like this one a part of your daily routine.

I love to think that animals and humans and plants and fishes and trees and stars and the moon are all connected.

—*Gloria Vanderbilt, artist*

Ask for an Unexpected Gift

When you want to set an intention, do it during the waxing moon, which is a time of growth and fulfillment. During this month, ask the energy of the moon and the universe to send you something unexpected every day for three days. Write a chant in your own words and repeat it three times on the first day. You can make it rhyme or not, and it can be as long or short as you like. Example: "Moon, moon, bring gift soon." This exercise will show you how well the moon's vibration is in touch with yours.

A gift does not have to be something that comes in a box with ribbons, of course—it could be something you found that was missing or a text from a friend you haven't heard from in ages. Don't look for things to force this to work. In fact, try to forget about it until it dawns on you that you just received something wonderful you never anticipated. Write down the gifts you receive that you were not expecting so you can be grateful for them. Also, document if you didn't receive anything at all. If this is the case, you probably need to continue to strengthen your connection with the moon's energy.

Summon a New Idea with a Candle Ritual

There's nothing like starting something new. It might be an invention you created, a relationship, a new chapter in your education, or a different career. Sometimes a new chapter begins before you even know what you want, in the form of sensing that you're ready for a change. If you need some inspiration, try this ritual.

You will need: four white candles, a toothpick (or something else with which to engrave your candles), and matches

1. Place the candles in fireproof containers or on plates.

2. Engrave one cardinal direction on each candle: N for north, E for east, etc. (You can engrave on the top of the candle, the sides, or anywhere you have room.)

3. Arrange the candles in a cross, with each candle at the appropriate place on the compass.

4. Now light the candles in this order: N, S, E, and W. As you light them, say over each candle, "Ideas from the north, ideas from the south," etc.

5. When all the candles are lit, sit for a few minutes and visualize creative energy coming to you from all directions.

6. Extinguish the candles. Write down any ideas that come to mind, or if you dream about a new adventure that night.

Track Your Full Moon Mood

The vibrational energy of the full moon affects everyone in different ways. Why not track your moods during full moons to see what it does to you? Check the circles that apply to you on this full moon. You'll do this exercise during each full moon to see if your mood stays the same or changes. *This full moon, I feel:*

○ Adventurous	○ Healthy	○ Magical
○ Anxious	○ Hopeful	○ Sexy
○ Athletic	○ Intuitive	○ So-So
○ Attractive	○ In love	○ Theatrical
○ Bored	○ In lust	○ Tired
○ Depressed	○ Jealous	○ Worried
○ Empowered	○ Lonely	○ _____
○ Generous	○ Lost	○ _____

Bless Your Home with Homemade Rose Water

The full moon in January represents freshness and sparkling newness. It's conducive to blessing your home, even if you've been living there for a while. It's a blessing for safety, happiness, and all good things you want in your abode. Your creative self will be at its fullest, so making homemade rose water should be easy and fun.

You will need: real rose petals and a jar or bowl; you can pluck a few from your garden if you have a rosebush that's in bloom now, or you could also just buy a few roses from a flower shop

1. Place the petals in the bowl or jar with some water. Give them a swish and you are ready to go.

2. Let your rose water sit on a windowsill or outside in the light of the moon while you write for a while. Express in words what you want your home to project (for example, happiness, prosperity, a family, a peaceful place, etc.). Write as many words as you want pertaining to your home.

3. If you live in a house, take your bowl and walk outside around the house and toss water at all the outside corners of the home. Think about what you wrote as you do this.

4. If you live in an apartment or you can't go outside, do an inside blessing. Take the water and stand in each corner of the apartment or even one room, hold the bowl out, and say, "I ask that this home be safeguarded with the power of the full moon and the powers that protect. And so it is." (You can also add any closing you like—"amen," "blessed be," etc.)

5. Discard the petals and water wherever you choose.

Change Your Luck with Herbal Magic

Feeling like things just haven't been going your way? A little herbal magic under the full moon can send your luck sky-high. Your intuitive self is overflowing as the moon's rich energy is ample. It will send out its powerful magic frequency to bring forth your request for good luck.

You will need: one basil leaf (dried or fresh) and a felt marker or pen

1. Take the basil leaf and write on it, *good luck*. On the night of a full moon (don't worry if it's cloudy), step outside and say, "Good luck will come so sweet and fast, upon this night my spell I cast." (If you don't want to use the word *spell*, say "my thought.")

2. Crumble or tear up the basil leaf and throw the pieces up toward the full moon. Let the wind take your intention out into the universe.

Write a Poem about Starting Over

When you feel like it's time to start anew in some area of your life, think about putting your feelings into words, either by journaling or by writing a poem. Expressing your feelings in this way gives you a starting point and a touchstone that you can use for motivation as you move through your journey. The following is just an example—feel free to use your own thoughts and words in your writing.

When I give myself permission to let go,

To dream a new reality for myself,

I give myself an unchartered future.

When I leave behind what's broken

And I embrace what's possible,

I am open, and I am free.

Minimize Your Obstacles at Work

As the moon continues its journey and begins to fade from view, it's time to take stock of what isn't working for you, and try to phase it out of your life so you can focus on your true self. Many of us run into obstacles in our career paths, so focus on that area of your life. When you're faced with a challenge at work, ask yourself:

1. Do I feel like I'm using my strengths at this job?

_____
_____
_____

2. Is there anything preventing me from being my absolute best at work?

_____
_____
_____

3. Am I doing work that is important to me?

_____
_____
_____

4. What is my priority in my career (money, status, creativity, etc.), and am I meeting it?

_____
_____
_____

5. What is my ideal work situation? Is that a realistic goal?

_____
_____
_____

You're going to spend a huge portion of your life working. A paycheck is important, but make sure that the effort you put into your job is serving you on a spiritual and personal level as well. If some or part of your job isn't working well for you, try to minimize or get rid of it during this moon phase. For example, if your weekly summary reports are tedious to create and aren't valuable on a week-to-week basis anyway, ask your boss if you can do them monthly instead. You will be a better person for it, and that positive energy is good for everyone around you!

Find the Right Partner for You with an Apple Ritual

This activity is useful if you're questioning a relationship or have more than one choice or are wondering who would be the best partner. Just like the waning moon appears to be reducing, this activity will narrow down your choices.

Grab any kind of apple. Hold it close to your heart and name your potential partner(s). Cut the apple (or bite into it) and remove some seeds. Assign one seed for each person in whom you are interested. Wet the seeds and stick them to your cheek (either one will do). Wait for them to fall off. The person represented by the last seed left is the best person for you. Record who fell off last, and at the next full moon, see if you have made any progress in this new or more stable relationship.

Discover Which Spirit Animals You Identify With

As the moon wanes and appears to be getting smaller, its energy is lower and more calming. This quiet atmosphere is an ideal time to identify and connect with your spirit or power animals, who can help you embrace your true self.

According to shamanic wisdom, a team of nine spirit animals accompanies each of us throughout life. Each one guides, protects, carries valuable messages, increases power, lends unique attributes, and offers a wealth of wisdom to help manifest experiences and healings.

Invite your spirit animals to show themselves during a meditation. Sit in a chair or your favorite place to meditate with your eyes closed. Picture a room with nine doors in a semicircle in front of you. In your mind, ask your spirit animals to come out. Do you see any? Does one stand out? Are any the same? Make a mental note of your favorite. Then open your eyes and make a physical note of the animal. Repeat this visualization at least three times throughout the day or night and see who stands out. One animal will show up repeatedly and stand out as a power animal.

Once you've identified your power animal, form a deeper connection and honor it by crafting a spiritual emblem in the space provided on this page. Drawing simple geometric shapes, a totem pole, or a shield can be fairly easy and fun. Feature your power animal in the center or at the top. Look up the meanings of spirit animals at www.spiritanimal.info.

Here are a few basic ones:

- **Bear:** strength
- **Bird:** freedom
- **Butterfly:** charm
- **Eagle:** vision
- **Horse:** power
- **Snake:** sensuality

February

Attract Abundance

Traditionally during this month, when winter storehouses were all but empty, our forebears anticipated or visualized coming seasons of plenty by seeking, acknowledging, and celebrating the first stir-rings of spring and the renewal of Earth's fertility. Despite the nearly bare cupboards, they readied for the coming year by performing rituals, such as blessing seeds and farming tools, baking seed cakes, and making candles to illuminate the coming months.

To harmonize with the energy of the moon in February, it's a good idea to clear your mind, emotions, and spirit to allow fresh inspiration to enter. This is the time to organize and clean for new enlightenment and new beginnings. Purify in preparation for the next cycle. Make room and make ready to invite blessings, attract health, and draw in prosperity—they are coming.

Decide What You Want

So many of us think we have a plan for our lives, but then we follow a course of action because we think we "should" or we feel we "have to," and everything else falls into place by default. The new moon is a time to take a fresh look at what you want for yourself and compare it against your current situation. Maybe this will be the first time you've ever thought about wanting something new or different for yourself!

The Law of Attraction tells us that you bring about what you think about. In other words, you will attract the things that you put your energy into—that's why it's so important to be clear on what you want! Make a list of the things you'd like to change, improve, or learn, and refer to it daily until it all comes to fruition. For example, if you want to move, start packing before your plans are in motion. Want a new job? Take a picture or draw a picture of a door with the words *old job* on it and burn it in a fireproof container. (You're representing an intention that when one door closes, another one opens.) You're empowering yourself to create the life you want!

Assess Your Feelings about Money

No matter how hard we work, most of us will always feel as though there's just never enough money. We convince ourselves that if money were no object, our lives would be much easier, completely carefree, and we could just enjoy ourselves. On the other hand, there are countless stories of wealthy people who are not happy, and in fact have cautioned others about believing that money solves every problem. Ask yourself these questions to discover how you feel about money:

• Is money a constant source of stress?

• Do you believe money can buy happiness?

• When do you spend money instead of saving? Is it for necessities only, or is making yourself feel good also a necessity?

• Do you work with a budget to keep yourself on track? Or is making a budget something new you might try under this lunar phase?

Are there ways that you can change your life right now to reflect your answers here? For example, how can you help others without spending a boatload of money? Is there a hobby or interest you want to develop to earn more money? The new moon is the time to try out these new patterns!

Clear Space
and Plan

The new moon is a time to clear space and nurture creative energy. Simply holding space and being receptive, open, poised to accept what is offered, and willing to heed messages from your inner knowing will open new paths and get things moving forward in the right direction. These questions can spark inspiration:

- What has come to a close recently that has cleared space for new projects?

- What have I been daydreaming or visualizing lately?

- What new opportunities have appeared?

- What new lens can I use to assess where I'm at right now?

- What new ways can I learn to open new doors in my life?

- What would I like to manifest right now?

- What three activities will help get the wheels of change turning?

Invite an Abundance of Peace to the Planet

The problems in the world can seem overwhelming sometimes, but that doesn't mean you shouldn't try to fix them. Try making subtle changes in how you think about world peace. Don't think antiwar; think pro-peace. Don't think about how horrible things are; focus on the good things around you. Concentrate on what a peaceful planet would look like to you. How would you like to see people act toward each other? What is your vision of world peace? Enhance your imagination as the moon grows in the sky. Write down your thoughts.

Enhance Your Wealth

On the night of a waxing moon, put nine copper coins (like pennies) under your front doormat. If you don't have an outdoor mat, put the money under an indoor mat near your front door. The coins will draw more money into your home thanks to their number and material. In numerology, 9 is a number of multiplication and abundance, and copper is a conductor. A waxing moon increases the energy of your intention to attract wealth, and you will be inviting prosperity through the door quickly. Leave the coins there until the day after the full moon.

With freedom, books, flowers, and the moon, who could not be happy?

—Oscar Wilde, author

Look for Signs of Abundance

A waxing moon is an uplifting time to send your intentions out and ask your higher power or source energy for things. This month, ask for more prosperity, however you define it. Then, every day for the next two weeks, write down any signs or symbols that indicate your wish is coming your way. For example, if you wanted to take a vacation that was more than you could afford, pay attention to the universe's ways of helping you. You may not even realize them at first, so be attentive. Maybe you suddenly see an ad online for an amazing discount on a hotel, or someone offers you a free place to stay in that city out of the blue. If it has to do with your thought, write it down. The more signs and symbols you see, the closer your wish is coming to being fulfilled.

Act Rich

Consider this: Some wealthy people are happy and some wealthy people are miserable—so it's important that you have a solid sense of self and spirituality prior to having a lot of loot! Under the waxing moon phase, answers will seem to flow to you easier because you are more enthusiastic. Right now, before you have all of your money, write down how your life will change.

• How will I give thanks when I have everything I want?

_____

_____

_____

• What will a typical day be like for me when I don't have to work for my money?

_____

_____

_____

• How will I treat others when I am wealthy?

_____

_____

_____

• Where will I live? What will my home be like?

_____

_____

_____

• What kind of car will I drive? Where will I buy my clothes?

_____

_____

_____

• What will I do for fun or to challenge myself?

_____

_____

_____

   Write your answers down so that you can refer to them in the future and keep yourself grounded when the money starts to roll in!

Attract $100 Into Your Life

Everything wants to grow during a waxing moon, so why not try to grow your bank account too? Try attracting $100 into your life. Write *$100* and today's date in the space here. Next to it, write a date ten days from now. Three times a day, look at the $100 you wrote down and think about what you want to do with that money and how you'll feel when you get it. What emotions will you have? Add an incantation after you are done writing. Make up your own or use this one: *I am attracting money with my power to ask, believe, and receive.* Do this for the next ten days, and then record how and when you got the $100.

/   /   /   /

Track Your Full Moon Mood

The vibrational energy of the full moon affects everyone in different ways. Why not track your moods during full moons to see what it does to you? Check the circles that apply to you on this full moon. You'll do this exercise during each full moon to see if your mood stays the same or changes. *This full moon, I feel:*

○ Adventurous	○ Healthy	○ Magical
○ Anxious	○ Hopeful	○ Sexy
○ Athletic	○ Intuitive	○ So-So
○ Attractive	○ In love	○ Theatrical
○ Bored	○ In lust	○ Tired
○ Depressed	○ Jealous	○ Worried
○ Empowered	○ Lonely	○ _____
○ Generous	○ Lost	○ _____

Plan Out
Your Fortune

Here's a fun activity that will get your creative juices flowing when it comes to attracting financial abundance into your life. Think about what you would do if you won the lottery tomorrow. Let's say you hit the jackpot for $50 million.

- Make a list of the people you would want to help financially and add how much you would give them.

_____

_____

_____

_____

_____

_____

_____

_____

_____

_____

_____

_____

- Now, how much would you spend on things that you want? Think about houses, cars, trips, boats, clothes, etc.

_____

_____

_____

_____

_____

_____

_____

_____

_____

_____

- What about charities? Which ones would you support and how much would you donate?

_____

_____

_____

_____

_____

_____

_____

Your answers will help you get a clear understanding about the reasons you are at-tracting money into your life in the first place.

Stay Focused On Your Goals

Staying focused on a goal is key to attracting abundance. Checking in on your goals using words and pictures is a handy tool to boost your energy, which allows the universe to hear your desires more clearly. For this exercise, think about a goal you're trying to achieve and write about it for four straight days. With the full moon, your thoughts should roll over the pages like a wave. Each day, write down one thing you have done to keep yourself on track.

For example, let's say your goal is to get a job at your dream company. Your four days might look like this:

Day 1:
I found out today who to contact about hiring.

Day 2:
I emailed my résumé to the right party.

Day 3:
I visualized myself working at a desk at this company.

Day 4:
I printed a picture of the company's office building and put it on my bulletin board so I can look at it daily.

Day 1:

Day 2:

Day 3:

Day 4:

Release Self-Doubt

As the moon begins to appear smaller this month, release habits and behaviors that don't serve you. One of the best things to send packing at this time is self-doubt. To reframe your mindset and build confidence, ask yourself these questions:

- What are three strengths that I have?

  _____
  _____
  _____

- What are three things I'm interested in learning?

  _____
  _____
  _____

- What are three things that I need to stop telling myself?

  _____
  _____
  _____

- What are three self-boosting statements I can recite each day?

  _____
  _____
  _____

Sell Items You No Longer Use

It's always kind to donate items you no longer need or want, but if you need a little extra cash and have some things of value, you may want to try to sell them online, at a garage sale, or via consignment. Look around and put together a pile of things you can sell. As the moon decreases in appearance, so can that pile of items you no longer use.

You will need: a green candle for profit-making vibrations, a toothpick, and matches

1. Carve a half moon or waxing moon on the top or side of the candle. (It should look like a D.)

2. As you light the candle, visualize all your unwanted items going to those who are looking for these particular things. Then:

   - Keep the candle near you if you are uploading pictures for an on-line store.

   - If you are having a garage sale, burn the candle while setting up.

   - Taking things to a store? Burn your candle before you go.

3. When your intuition tells you to extinguish your candle, do so.

Stop Recurring Nightmares

Do you have a recurring nightmare or bad dream? Take advantage of the waning moon's power to get rid of that dream once and for all. But don't be too quick to let it depart—you need to heed the warning it brings. Whether these dreams are trying to get you to resolve something from the past, change something in the present, or plan for something in the future, they usually have a purpose.

When trying to analyze your dreams, think symbolism. A bear chasing you in your dream doesn't mean a bear is literally going to run you down at the grocery store. But it may mean that someone who is strong and aggressive is trying to get in touch with you. Dream situations can also symbolize other things, depending on your personal feelings on the topic. If you love flowers, a dream that includes them could indicate happiness. But if you detest flowers, it could be pointing out a negative situation.

Write down your recurring dreams in detail and track how often they visit you. If your dreams start to change for the better as you understand them more fully, that could mean you are working through problems. If they get worse, you may need to keep searching for their meaning, or start addressing some issues you have been ignoring.

By journaling your dreams, you should find that your recurring nightmares make their point and eventually stop.

Replace Negative Words
with Positive Ones

Words are thoughts that can both take shape as visual symbols (through letters) and become auditory vibrational sounds with their own energy patterns. That's why words are so powerful! During the waning moon, release pessimistic language and replace it with uplifting, loving, and prosperous words.

According to spiritual leader Emmet Fox, the Law of Substitution suggests that the only way to get rid of a problematic thought is to substitute another better one. Instead of trying to fight a negative thought, turn your attention to and focus your energy on a constructive idea. For example, if you're concerned about a health issue, replace words such as *disease* and *illness* with *fitness, heartiness, soundness,* and *wholeness* to add positive energy to the healing process. Swap "I feel so tired all the time" to "I'll get more sleep so I feel more energetic." Compose, write, and speak affirmations with these types of words instead.

Negative Words   →   Positive Words

March

Improve
Your Intuition

The gentle whispered promise of potential from the last moon cycle begins to shift into action and show up in new forms in March. Earth is warming up and awakening anew. The wind blows in refreshing air, waters run freely from snowmelt, frozen ground starts to soften, crocuses push their way up through soil, sap starts to flow, and earthworms begin to emerge, heralding the return of birds.

Synchronizing with the energy of March's moon cycle calls for perking up perceptions, yielding to imagination, tuning in to the flow of emotions, and tapping in to and trusting intuition to lead you to your next great breakthrough. Your intuitive intelligence is like the wind moving through the trees—it may not be visible, but you can see the metaphorical leaves rustle and realize the power of its effects in bridging spiritual heavenly realms and material earthly realities. Tune in and connect to the potent force within (what some simply call your spirit).

Contemplate the Spring Season

When spring arrives and we have emerged from the winter, the new moon calls us to think about starting again. What's on your mind as you walk toward a new season? Do you think of budding flowers or the possibilities of launching innovative opportunities? Draw what spring means to you, and compare it with your thoughts about other seasons.

List Your Favorite Spell-Casting Tools and Ingredients

Thanks to an increased ability to concentrate, the new moon is a good time to collect your favorite items for divination, spells, rituals, and meditation. Put a lot of thought into your collection and make a list of your favorite candle colors, your favorite incense, your preferred oracle deck, your most-loved statues, and other things you like to put on your altar or personal area. In the future, looking back at these pages will bring awareness to what in your life has changed and what's stayed the same. Every new moon, make a new list and compare.

Discover Yourself Through Tarot Cards

The new moon is a powerful time to think about boosting your intuition. Go through your tarot cards and take a look to see who you think you are and who you aspire to be. Choose one card that you relate to intuitively. With the onset of the new moon, own and be proud of the personality you have.

CARD	MEANING
The Fool (0)	Is pure and welcomes new beginnings
The Magician (I)	Shows willpower
The High Priestess (II)	Hears the inner voice or has strong intuition
The Empress (III)	Shows signs of beauty and caring
The Emperor (IV)	Shows an ability to rule
The Hierophant (V)	Teaches things holy and gives blessings
The Lovers (VI)	Is committed in love
The Chariot (VII)	Is optimistic, enjoys experiencing life
Strength (VIII)	Represents passion, fear of the unknown, balance
The Hermit (IX)	Enjoys being alone; is wise, serious, eccentric
Wheel of Fortune (X)	Is lucky, successful; represents new circumstances
Justice (XI)	Is balanced, fair, intelligent
The Hanged Man (XII)	Regenerates themselves before they move on
Death (XIII)	Connotes a rebirth to move forward
Temperance (XIV)	Is a team player; represents dreams now coming true
The Devil (XV)	Shows evil, material obsession; often makes wrong choices
The Tower (XVI)	Represents liberation of insecurity
The Star (XVII)	Understands the cosmos
The Moon (XVIII)	Shows intuition; not getting lost in themselves
The Sun (XIX)	Shows great pleasure or delight
Judgment (XX)	Has discernment, healing, transformation
The World (XXI)	Is a high achiever

Treat Yourself

Every now and then, we have to treat ourselves in order to engage the mind and spirit, and identify and address our needs. To someone who has been burning the candle at both ends, a spa day offers a much-needed time of rest and reflection. What about other things that help to lift your spirits? Consider…

- **New shoes**: Running shoes, heels, flip-flops, whatever makes you feel great

- **Vintage items**: Tarot cards, crystals, or incense that help you connect with your spirit guides

- **Clothes**: Something that shows off your recent diet and exercise efforts, or clothes for relaxation

- **Books**: Look for something that can bring joy and peace to your life

The moon appears to be brighter and more polished, and this exercise helps you follow suit. Keep in mind that money is never wasted if it's spent on things that are good for the soul. The moon shines at this lunar phase, and so will your spirit. Jot down some ideas on how you can treat yourself.

Imagine
a Past Life

The waxing moon is best for this exercise, as your time-travel memory is elevated. Sometimes the full moon is too intense a time to try this, so stick with the waxing phase for past life remembrances. Other moon phases are excellent for past life matters, but when it comes to writing about your gut feelings, this phase nails it. Follow these steps for a guided visualization:

1. Picture an old black train or locomotive with travelers inside. You can't see yourself yet, but you are a passenger.

2. The train pulls into a foggy station and you walk down the steps onto the lonely platform. What do you see? Do you appear like a character from a time before trains were even created, like an ancient Egyptian or an Atlantean? What do you look like—man or woman? How old? Write down as many details as you can.

3. How does that person make you feel? Are you alone? Do you have children, animals, luggage? Who are you?

Test Your ESP Skills with Zener Cards

Many people don't know there are fun and interesting ESP tests online, such as the one at https://psychicscience.org/esp1. The test was invented by J.B. Rhine and Karl Zener from Duke University's psychology department and contains five symbols (star, circle, wave, cross, and square) on twenty-five cards. You have to choose which symbols are on cards turned facedown. The odds and instructions are explained. Try this at the waxing phase of the moon and compare the results to other phases to see when you are more accurate.

The more you do this, the more you will get a feel for it and potentially improve. Try to remember how you were feeling and your circumstances when your sessions were more accurate. You can also buy or make your own deck of Zener cards if you like, so you don't have to do it on a screen.

Try Scrying or Gazing

Scrying is the process of gazing into a reflective surface—such as a mirror, a crystal ball, or a cup of water—where you can see images of the past, present, and future. You can also do this by gazing into a candle flame. It's akin to daydreaming with your eyes open. It is an art and takes practice, but it's worth a try to see what you experience. Ancient people did scrying when the moon was on the increase, or waxing. They thought the impressions would be more plentiful and would appear more quickly.

To try it out, pick a clear object like a crystal or cup of water. Get into a very peaceful state via meditation or relaxation and stare at the object. See if you can discern any images.

Track Your Full Moon Mood

The vibrational energy of the full moon affects everyone in different ways. Why not track your moods during full moons to see what it does to you? Check the circles that apply to you on this full moon. You'll do this exercise during each full moon to see if your mood stays the same or changes. *This full moon, I feel:*

○ Adventurous	○ Healthy	○ Magical
○ Anxious	○ Hopeful	○ Sexy
○ Athletic	○ Intuitive	○ So-So
○ Attractive	○ In love	○ Theatrical
○ Bored	○ In lust	○ Tired
○ Depressed	○ Jealous	○ Worried
○ Empowered	○ Lonely	○ _____
○ Generous	○ Lost	○ _____

Honor the Moon with Mugwort

Artemis is the lunar goddess who beckons us to journey with her into a magical realm and leave the material behind…if only for a phase. Mugwort aids in dream and trance work and can make your dreams fill with visions of the future.

Some herbalists prefer to reap mugwort (which can grow in many climates) near the full moon, when the energies are concentrated in the above-ground portions of the plant. Mugwort can be burned as incense or put into a pouch and kept near your night-stand at night to conjure up dreams of divination. You can find mugwort at herbal stores, order it online, or buy it in incense form.

Dice Prophecies

The grounds in March are warming and the full moon brings out your intuitive nature. So why not warm up those dice and get a few answers? This quick method uses two dice but advanced systems use three. Concentrate on your question while shaking the dice in your hand and toss. Add the numbers of the two dice together to interpret your answer. Roll three times total for a bigger picture. Here are interpretations of the numbers:

2: Harmony, balance	3: Jealousy, scandal	4: Turn to others for guidance
5: Birth, marriage, union	6: Money issues, loss— try to stay positive nonetheless	7: Don't neglect friends and family; they will help
8: New love or a higher level of commitment with someone	9: Possible bad energy coming— pay attention; it can be avoided	10: Success and happiness are coming; be more social
11: Change is coming, so adapt, meditate, rest	12: Your finances are improving; believe in your goals	

Don't forget to jot down your results!

Spend a Day Following Your Intuition

As the moon's glow lessens, so in the lunar spirit, you let go of assumptive thought. Take a full day (or at least half) and follow only your gut feeling. Release your normal routine from your thinking. Pardon your mind the old routines and patterns. As the moon appears like it's decreasing, so should your mental navigational system. Do things uniquely. Don't make life-changing decisions, but have fun with small choices like what to eat and how to spend your time.

For example, maybe a store has something on display that you really don't need. Since it's only $5 and your intuition is saying "buy it," you do so. Later that day someone comes over who needs just that item, and you have done them a favor. Or maybe you feel a need to help someone you never really cared for. After you lend them a hand, that person shares a piece of information that really helps you in some way, and it's a win-win situation.

At the end of the day, see how the experience made you feel. Make notes here so you can remember everything.

Practice Psychic Etiquette

The moon's waning vibration is prompting us to release thoughts that don't serve us, such as those that are selfish or judgmental. This is an exercise about identifying these thoughts as they relate to spiritual advisors; then you can let go of them, or perhaps encourage others to let go of them.

When you are dealing with intuitive readers, healers, or spiritual advisors, remember that these people make their living helping others and should be treated with respect. When you buy a block of time from someone for a healing or an appointment regarding forecasting the future or spiritual counseling, these professionals should be treated the same way you'd treat a doctor or financial advisor. Put yourself in their shoes and write down five things that would frustrate you if you were (or maybe you are) a psychic reader, healer, or spiritual counselor.

1.

2.

3.

4.

5.

Identify Who Guides Your Intuition

You don't have to be a professional to have intuition. I believe my intuition comes from my spirit. Other people find their intuitive thoughts come from channeling information, God, the goddess, a higher power, or a source energy. The moon is in more of a quiet mode now, so try some quiet contemplation. Reflect on where you think your psychic emotions come from and how they can increase with the waxing and full moon. Who or what in your opinion is behind it all? These questions may help you decide:

• Do you pray or meditate before working with forms of divination?

_____

_____

_____

_____

• Do you suddenly get intuitive thoughts when you're not even trying to?

_____

_____

_____

_____

• Do you have dreams that foretell the future?

_____

_____

_____

_____

• Are people telling you that your "gut feeling" is usually right?

_____

_____

_____

Write down where you think your intuitive side comes from. When you have found that answer, it's easier to tap in to your psychic self when you need to. Before you know it, you will be doing it without concentrating as much.

_____

_____

_____

_____

_____

_____

_____

_____

Analyze Your Superstitions

Superstitions can be funny little beliefs (holding your breath when passing a cemetery) or long-held fears (breaking a mirror). Which of these superstitions do you believe or practice?

- ○ Saying "God bless you" after someone sneezes
- ○ Throwing spilled salt over your shoulder
- ○ Avoiding black cats
- ○ Not walking under ladders
- ○ Keeping umbrellas closed inside
- ○ Picking up pennies for luck
- ○ Carrying a rabbit's foot
- ○ Believing bad things happen in sets of threes
- ○ Fearing certain numbers, like 13 or 666
- ○
- ○
- ○
- ○
- ○

If you have some superstitions you want to let go of, this moon phase is the time to do so. Write down what happens when you actually encounter a black cat or you forget your rabbit's foot. I bet it isn't the outcome you think!

April

Reset
Your Priorities

During this spring moon cycle, when the earth is born anew and bursting forth with enthusiasm, it's time for you to do the same. This is an advantageous period to set intentions, which, like seeds, will grow and eventually come to fruition.

Reinvention is the key to positive change in your life. Now is the time to re-evaluate, reprioritize, redesign, and shape a bright new beginning that will encourage growth in the coming months. Start by engaging the fresh perspectives you happened upon last month, and mix them with this month's constructive moon energy to reassess old habits and set new goals.

Reflect briefly on the past, but don't dwell there. Procrastination has no place now with energy on the rise. Take stock and move promptly into the fertile present. Affirm your current self and situation, then give yourself permission to put ideas into motion, take action, and move forward toward a more fulfilled future...confidently, courageously realizing your full potential.

"Box Up" Worrisome Thoughts

Because the new moon brings about positive changes, this is the time to sort out thoughts that are weighing heavily on your mind and put some of them to rest. Sometimes we've been focused on a negative thought for so long, it becomes a belief, and we need a wake-up call to stop torturing ourselves with it. For example, long-standing worries about money might stick around even after you've established your career and are doing well financially. In this example, you could ask yourself whether cash flow is still a valid concern. If you determine that it's not a reality-based fear, visualize yourself boxing it up and recycling or donating it, along with other old things that have no place in your current life. Take a few moments to write down worrisome thoughts that you can get rid of this month.

_____

_____

_____

_____

_____

_____

_____

Clear Your Chakras

The new moon is a time for reawakening, so let's clear your chakras in order to renew your body, mind, and spirit. You can do a quick chakra clearing yourself, or visit a professional energy worker or acupuncturist to do it for you. To do a quick cleanse at home, follow these steps:

1. Lie down on your bed or sofa.

2. Close your eyes and see a blue light (the color of healing) come from the bottom of your feet and gradually move to the top of your head.

3. Now see that glow of blue turn to clear or white.

4. Stay in the white light, which acts as a spiritual shield from negative energy, for a few seconds. Then see the light fade and get up.

   Jot down how you felt before and after this process.

_____

_____

_____

_____

_____

Listen to Nature at Night

During this phase of the moon, get out in nature and let it inspire you to grow and expand your spiritual side. Try to appreciate what nature offers at nighttime. Take a walk one evening as the moon is waxing. Note the changes in the moon and what your experience of nature is at nighttime. What do you hear? How is the smell of the evening different from daytime? Do you have fears in the dark, or do you welcome it? There are no right or wrong answers; just notice your own personal experience.

Determine What Inspires You

We all need to feel inspired and motivated—without these forces, life is empty of hope. But what inspires you may not feel inspirational at all to the next person. Each of us finds beauty in our own way, so don't blindly accept what you see on social media as "inspirational." Write down the things that make you feel like you want to be the best you can be. Consider the following list, adding or changing items to reflect what inspires you.

O Nature

O Community (church, friends, volunteer organizations)

O Music, literature, art

O Physical exercise

O Family

O Animals

O

O

O

O

O

O

Plan a Trip

The waxing moon allows you to engage in its energy to bring your dreams to fruition. Nothing is off the table during this time of dreaming. For this activity, think about where you'd like to travel. For now, don't put limits of money, time, or distance on your destinations. Where would you go? How long would you stay? Would you travel in luxury or would you prefer to "rough it"? Write down five places you'd like to go and describe those trips in detail.

1.

2.

3.

4.

5.

Balance Brain Neurotransmitters with Essential Oils

During this waxing lunar cycle, when the moon is moving toward fullness, our brain tends to be heavily influenced by serotonin. Serotonin is a calming and uplifting neurotransmitter that assists us in regulating mood, social behavior, appetite and digestion, sleep, and memory. Moreover, it helps us to focus on work, and organize and prioritize our to-do lists.

Essential oils can have a powerful impact on the release, uptake, and availability of neurotransmitters through our sense of smell. Bergamot, lavender, citrus, clary sage, and Roman and German chamomile help optimize serotonin levels and restore balance in our limbic system.

Select one essential oil from this list. Use a diffuser, spray, or steam inhalation to safely breathe in your chosen essential oil. Pay attention as you go about your daily activities and note any effects you notice.

ASPECT OF YOUR BEING	ESSENTIAL OIL SUGGESTIONS	QUESTIONS TO ASK YOURSELF
Physical body	Patchouli, vetiver, nutmeg	What is my body saying? What does it need?
Emotional	Jasmine, orange, neroli, cardamom	What emotions are foremost? How have I processed them?
Mental	Rosemary, ginger, pine, lemon	What thoughts are dominating my thinking? What habitual mental patterns need to be modified?
Collective/Relational	Bergamot, lavender, myrrh, grapefruit	What am I grateful for?
Expressive	Peppermint, basil, hyssop, clove	In what ways can I be more authentic?
Intuitive	Clary sage, frankincense, Melissa, German chamomile	How can I better listen to and trust my intuition?
Spiritual	Angelica, tuberose, rose, helichrysum, sandalwood	What puts me in a state of bliss connected to Divine Mystery?

Track Your Full Moon Mood

The vibrational energy of the full moon affects everyone in different ways. Why not track your moods during full moons to see what it does to you? Check the circles that apply to you on this full moon. You'll do this exercise during each full moon to see if your mood stays the same or changes. *This full moon, I feel:*

○ Adventurous   ○ Healthy   ○ Magical

○ Anxious   ○ Hopeful   ○ Sexy

○ Athletic   ○ Intuitive   ○ So-So

○ Attractive   ○ In love   ○ Theatrical

○ Bored   ○ In lust   ○ Tired

○ Depressed   ○ Jealous   ○ Worried

○ Empowered   ○ Lonely   ○ _____

○ Generous   ○ Lost   ○ _____

Write Down Your Life's Journey So Far

The full moon gives us a lot of energy, so this is a good time to write your life story—but the caveat is that you have to do it in under three hundred words. To some people, this will sound like a lot of writing; to others, it will seem like barely enough space to scratch the surface—but that's the point! Try not to get pulled into the details of any one event. Pretend you have to tell a total stranger about your life, from the beginning until this very moment, in under three minutes. This is meant to remind you of the highlights of your life, just as the moon is at its highest energy.

Heal the Planet

When the full moon is beaming down with its brightest frequency, you may find yourself filled with thoughts that concern the greater good, such as the state and future of the earth. Some people find their thoughts frantically pinging around during this time of high energy. Put some of those thoughts on paper with this stress-relieving exercise.

Draw our world in your own style using the circle here. On or near it, write words that you feel will replenish, help, and protect the planet. You can also add shapes, symbols, or images that are meaningful to you.

Give a Compliment to a Stranger

So little goes so far; a compliment, a smile, or a nod of approval, especially to a stranger or someone not expecting it, can make someone's day. A waning moon whispers, "It's not all about you."

Release your selfishness and say something nice, or just be patient with someone you might have otherwise been frustrated with. At the grocery store, is the older lady in front of you quiet and looking lonely? How about saying something like, "I love those earrings," or "You have a nice smile"?

Does she look grumpy? How about sending a smile her way? You really don't realize what you have the power to do with simple, loving body language. Try it and release yourself from being self-absorbed. Write down some ideas of ways you can compliment others.

Don't worry if you're making waves simply by being yourself. The moon does it all the time.

—Scott Stabile, author

Sketch Your Feelings

Use the space on this page to release what is weighing heavily on your body, mind, and spirit. Watch the waning moon as it expressively lets go, and follow suit. Mimic this phase, and the energy in and of itself will help you let loose. Expand your emotional intelligence by drawing a picture of what a current feeling looks like each day over a three-day period. Gather some colored pencils, paints, markers, or crayons and draw your emotion. You don't need any special artistic talent. Turn your judgment off and give yourself permission to express freely. Let the feeling flow through you, into your hand, and out onto the page. Simply doodling or splattering paint is fine as long as you let your emotion guide what you create. Compare the three days' creations, reflect, and journal your insights.

Use a Dowsing Pendulum to Intuitively Align Your Spring Agenda

The waning moon in April is a good time for accomplishing spring cleaning and giving yourself a fresh start. This includes reviewing, re-evaluating, and revising resolutions made at the beginning of the year. Clean up and rearrange your objectives by learning to calibrate and use a pendulum.

Based on the idea that the body doesn't lie, a pendulum is an ancient tool for accessing inner wisdom and getting answers not readily available through conscious awareness. A simple one can be made by attaching any moderately heavy object, such as a small washer or a ring, to an 8" piece of string. Ask it some simple yes-or-no questions, and take note of what it shows you for each response so you know what "yes" and "no" look like. Then ask the pendulum yes-or-no questions related to your goals, and write down the responses to each question.

Cut Back on Three Unhealthy Foods

The waning moon is a good time to modify your diet. Developing a conscious relationship with your digestion by paying close attention to foods that stress your digestive system is an important first step. Once you do this, it's much easier to make positive changes to support better digestion. Ask yourself these questions:

- What three foods have I noticed are negatively impacting my digestion?

1.

_____

_____

2.

_____

_____

3.

_____

_____

- How will cutting back/eliminating these foods improve my digestion? My overall health?

_____

_____

_____

_____

_____

- What small steps can I take to reduce my consumption and accomplish long-term success and healthy change?

_____

_____

_____

_____

_____

- What other healthier options might I substitute when I am craving these foods?

_____

_____

_____

_____

_____

Make a Bracelet to Remind You of Your Priorities

Keeping your priorities in mind can be a challenge. Crafting two bracelets, one for current priorities and the other for future goals, can help keep priorities in the front of your mind and be a conduit for positive change. The luminous moon is appearing to discharge some of its light; that's where the second bracelet takes center stage. Create both, and wear the one that suits your mood the best (or wear them at the same time).

1. Plan and illustrate your design, selecting colors and materials that symbolize your goals. The bracelets can be simple, natural, and inexpensive or elaborate and more costly. Consider alphabet beads to spell out a word; some sort of code to embed a secret message; charms or stamped metal to represent a thought or totem; or textiles for weaving. Decide on fishing line, thread, jute, elastic string, ribbons, leather, or wire to construct your design.

2. Next, gather the supplies you need. Old jewelry can be dismantled for parts. Some other places to look for supplies are nature, tag sales, or craft or bead shops. You can also try thrift, resale, and vintage stores.

3. Meditate on your intention while assembling and wearing the bracelets.

May

Bolster Creative Instincts

In midspring, the May moon cycle embodies the height of fertility, fast-growing change, and the energy of total emergence. There's wakefulness now. Flora is in full bloom, expressing joy, exuding life-giving energy, and generating potent healing medicines.

Creativity is the essence of being; the enchantment of life. During this month's moon, when inner capabilities shine through and flourish, it's a great time to explore and celebrate your inner muse and the flowering of life. You are ripe to create and birth blossoms of brilliance, so adopt a youthful curiosity and commune with the source of your imagination.

To align with the power of this creative moon, revel in play, delight in pleasure and sensuality, dance in the moonlight, and rejoice in the connection to the web of all life that magically connects us to generative abundance.

Jump-Start Your Creative Side

The new moon brings the opportunity for fresh perspective and imagination. This is the time to start a project or jump into an activity you've been itching to try. For inspiration, ask yourself:

1. What did I want to be when I was a child? How close am I to that as an adult? How and why did that vision change?

_____

_____

_____

_____

_____

2. What are my strengths and gifts?

_____

_____

_____

_____

_____

3. Do I want to share my strengths with others? How can I do that?

_____

_____

_____

_____

_____

_____

4. What do I need to do to feel my best?

_____

_____

_____

_____

_____

5. What kind of environment sparks my creative side?

_____

_____

_____

_____

This exercise should help you nurture the often-forgotten open and "fun" side of your mind!

Draw a Dragon

Imagine that you're out walking on a foggy night during the new moon when suddenly a formidable dragon appears. Having shown herself, she now considers you dragon kin. Dragons connect with healing, as well as ancestors, because she can awaken you to the restoration and honoring of your body, mind. and/or spirit. The new moon, which shows little if any light, still watches over the night and the creatures that stir below. Since our imaginations prod us to be resourceful like the dragon, it's an ideal time to fashion a dragon picture.

Study the dragon you see and draw this mysterious, fierce, magical creature that has just revealed herself to you. Is she a fire, water, earth, air, or some other type of dragon? Talk with her. Write down any messages she passes along. If she doesn't send an explicit message, interpret the symbolism present in her characteristics to understand her message/gift.

Write Your Own Blessing

Once in a while, at an event of some kind, it might be nice to say a blessing of sorts— but often, no one knows what to do or feels comfortable stepping up. With this exercise, you can offer your services! Since you will likely not know what everyone's spiritual belief may be, keep your blessing nondenominational.

The light of the waxing moon fills us with thoughtfulness and appreciation, and it's a meaningful time to honor your sharing nature and put some thought into dedications or good intentions that you could use at a variety of events. Fill in these blanks to get started or write your own blessing.

- Bless this_____
  and the hands that helped to create it.

- May positive energy fill this

  _____

  with love and safety.

- With joy in our hearts, we say thank you
  for_____.

- In the spirit of the universe and all things
  good, _____.

Anoint a Candle for Divination Enhancement

As it makes its way to the full phase, the waxing moonlight offers great potential for seeing into your future. If you don't like divining under a full moon because the energy is too intense, do it during a waxing moon. No matter what style of divination you use (tarot cards, scrying into a crystal ball), do it alongside this anointed candle to add a little more power.

You will need: a white or purple candle (remember, white bestows the vibration of purity and power, and the vibration of purple is associated with psychic energy and insight), a pinch of salt, two drops of violet oil, two drops of wisteria oil, and two drops of lilac oil (or you can use your own special combination of essential oils that promotes your intuitive abilities)

1. You can dab each ingredient separately near the wick, or combine the ingredients and dab on the candle wherever you like.

2. Hold the candle in your hands and turn it while thinking about what you want.

3. Now light the candle and concentrate on the form of divination you will do.

Honor Women

The concept of the Triple Goddess encompasses the three phases of womanhood: Maiden, Mother, and Crone; these also coincide with the phases of the moon (waxing, full, and waning) and the seasons (spring, summer, fall/winter). Follow these steps to honor all women:

1. Gather some friends together during the waxing moon and pay homage to the full cycle of the moon and womanhood—all of it is to be celebrated!

2. The ritual can be as simple as sitting in a circle, joining hands and energies, and invoking the Triple Goddess. For example, you could say:

   "We welcome you, Triple Goddess, into this circle of women, and ask that you lift our spirits and hearts and remind us of our strengths and true beauty."

3. You may want to share what each of you feels it is to be women at different stages of life, and how each of you welcomes different phases.

4. Close your ceremony by thanking the goddess for her presence and power.

Perform a Journal Activation Spell

This activity will help you bless and activate this journal. In the makeshift compass on this page, make a representation of yourself facing east, a direction that denotes clarity and bringing forth ideas. (You can literally draw yourself, or simply use an X, a star, or any other symbol.) The sun comes up in the east, and your thoughts and love of yourself, which you are trying to achieve via this journal, will also take flight. If you want, you can add enhancements in your drawing, like a candle. Draw an altar if the mood strikes you. Look down at your picture and say:

"Oh, waxing moon's shining light,

I activate my journal's flight.

Transformation, goals, self-love.

It is below as is above."

Ponder what you have written so far in this journal and anticipate what you may be considering in the future.

If you like, use the compass in other rituals and spells. Facing certain compass directions can make us feel one way or the other. Try facing each direction and write down how each direction makes you feel.

Each direction signifies a different theme:

- **North**: Power, organizing, intuition, integrity

- **South**: Artistic endeavors, emotion, self-control

- **East**: Renewal, hope, love, spirituality

- **West**: Gateways, completion, inner wisdom

You can stand or sit on the floor or a chair in the middle of a room with your eyes open or closed. If you venture outside, it's important you are safe or you will tense up and the observation will not be accurate.

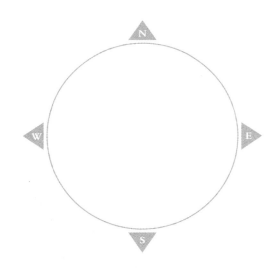

Track Your Full Moon Mood

The vibrational energy of the full moon affects everyone in different ways. Why not track your moods during full moons to see what it does to you? Check the circles that apply to you on this full moon. You'll do this exercise during each full moon to see if your mood stays the same or changes. *This full moon, I feel:*

○ Adventurous	○ Healthy	○ Magical
○ Anxious	○ Hopeful	○ Sexy
○ Athletic	○ Intuitive	○ So-So
○ Attractive	○ In love	○ Theatrical
○ Bored	○ In lust	○ Tired
○ Depressed	○ Jealous	○ Worried
○ Empowered	○ Lonely	○ _____
○ Generous	○ Lost	○ _____

Put On Some Silver and Shine

The full moon mirrors light, just as silver reflects an enchanting glow when you wear it. If you have always preferred silver (choosing it over gold), it may be that moon connection. The frequency of silver gives it a healing element. Combine that with the vibration of the full moon and your power of restoration is heightened. An added bonus is that silver protects you from negativity, as it reflects it away. During this full moon, adorn yourself with your favorite silver jewelry and make note if you become uplifted by the magical lunar luster it bestows.

Make a Decision Using Automatic Writing

Automatic writing is the practice of writing words in an unedited, free-flowing way to gain direct guidance from a place outside of your conscious awareness. It's a great method for obtaining clarity and making intuitive decisions.

1. Think of a question that you want guidance about—the more emotional, the better. Keep it simple. Be clear.

2. Jot down your question on the next page. Address it to an angel, a spirit guide, or your soul.

3. Relax your body and empty your mind through meditation, mindfulness, self-hypnosis, breathing, or yoga.

4. Allow the writing to flow spontaneously. Stay relaxed and don't judge or edit what you write. Look away if that helps.

5. Be patient and take as much time as you need. Stay present, calm, and centered.

6. Once you've stopped, review and interpret the information.

Use Artistic Endeavors to Calm and Cure

Try as we might, stress finds its way into even the most peaceful lives. The act of creating can help to soothe anxiety, anger, and depression. Creating is not just for professional artists—we all have something to express in an artistic manner. Think about these options:

- **Coloring:** All you need is a picture and colored pencils, markers, or crayons.

- **Sketching:** Use pencil, pen, charcoal, or chalk.

- **Writing:** Journal or write a story or poem.

- **Photography:** You can use your camera phone or a good old-fashioned handheld camera to capture moments, events, or nature.

- **Singing:** Belting out your favorite tunes (or writing new ones) is particularly good for the soul!

- **Playing music:** Play a piano, guitar, drums, spoons—whichever instrument speaks to you.

- **Decorating or redecorating:** Simply moving furniture or hanging a new wall decoration can make the energy in your space feel completely different.

Don't worry about the outcome—just start creating and let the work take care of itself.

Dance to Spark Your Artistic Side

Dancing is a great way to boost your creativity levels. It's invigorating and you can shake the blues, creative stagnation, and imagination shutdown right out into the universe! The lunar phase of waning helps you kick (maybe literally) any negative vibrations blocking your creativity right out of your life. Free your right brain (which is your creative side). If it's possible, dance outside in the moonlight! Later, document how you feel after a dance session to remind yourself.

Clear Your Home's Energy with Feng Shui

Look into the ancient art more on your own time and jot down notes and remedies of interest.

May's moon phases bring us creativity and growth. That said, you want to make sure the energy around you is open and ready to accept these blessings. During the waning moon, when the moon's energy encourages release, let go of any negative vibes in your home using feng shui. Feng shui is the Chinese art of placing certain items in certain spots based on how energy (or chi) moves around them.

Following are a few quick cures for keeping bad vibes out of your home:

- Place a bagua mirror (a round mirror surrounded by an octagonal frame) on the outside of your house above your front door to deflect bad luck away from your home.

- Hang wind chimes or faceted crystals in key spots to disperse chi. Plus, the sounds drive away contrary forces.

- Always remove dead or dying plants and flowers in the house; it subconsciously reminds us of death and dying. That's why some people never have potpourri or dried flowers in their homes. Always opt for live fresh plants and flowers.

Rid Yourself of Artistic Blocks

Align yourself to the waning moon if you want to transform those artistic blocks into stepping stones. Try this simple guided meditation.

1. Picture a tree with a little fairy door at the bottom, a gateway that opens onto a path, or an archway covered with flowers and foliage. Pick one of the three and draw it in the following space. This is your portal.

2. To the left or right of your portal is a bench. Draw it as well.

3. Now close your eyes or stare at your drawing and see yourself in the image, carrying a backpack or tote filled with items. You don't have to determine what the items are; it's whatever is stopping you from creating—that's all you need to know. Put the bag down on the bench and walk through the portal.

4. Once you walk through, what positive things do you see? What do you do? How do you feel?

5. When the mood strikes you, turn around and come back through. Your items are gone; they were things that no longer served you anyway. Now or the next day, see if you can get back your artistic flow. Can't? Do it again!

Challenge Your Horoscope Assumptions

Each astrology sign has its strengths and challenges. As the moon lets go of her bright light, consider letting go of your zodiac assumptions. According to stereotypical astrological attributes, which ones are spot on and which don't seem to fit your personality? If you don't fit the mold for a certain sign, maybe something else is at play. Perhaps as you get older, you are more connected to your rising sign, or your Moon sign seems more accurate. Think about contacting a professional astrologer and asking for insights. "One size fits all" may not fit you anymore!

SIGN	POSITIVE ATTRIBUTES	CHALLENGING ATTRIBUTES
Aries	Ambitious, courageous	Impatient, self-involved
Taurus	Practical, creative	Stubborn, possessive
Gemini	Energetic, free	Restless, confused
Cancer	Sensitive, intuitive	Moody, controlling
Leo	Friendly, bold	Childlike, demanding
Virgo	Organized, industrious	Arrogant, perfectionist
Libra	Harmonious, friendly	Insecure, indecisive
Scorpio	Empathetic, passionate	Jealous, brooding
Sagittarius	Openhearted, adventurous	Rebellious, undiplomatic
Capricorn	Ambitious, quick-minded	Self-centered, critical
Aquarius	Easygoing, independent	Distant, opinionated
Pisces	Sensitive, intuitive	Overemotional, overindulgent

June

Avert Harmful Energy

In June, a month of long days and short nights, we experience the last moon of spring as solar energy is heating up, days lengthen, and we celebrate the peak of solar power. The world around continues to transform. Crops and herbs grow in leaps and bounds; hives are full of honey as bees take advantage of the long days and bountiful blooms.

As the life-giving solar force heightens vibrations, fortifies resolve, and builds strength, we are impelled to make hay while the sun shines! Infused with warmth from the extended hours of daylight, nights are short, fragrant, and enthralling, packed with all manner of intense sensory and dreamy midsummer experiences.

At this turning point midway through the year, the moon calls us back to what is most meaningful at deeper levels. In the chaotic hyper-productive peak of solstice light, it's an ideal time to pause and turn inward. Take a beat, review intentions, reorient strategies, and reset the compass route to what nourishes the soul and not just the ego. This will raise your vibration. When we turn up our frequency to a positive channel, negative forces can't filter through. It's akin to wearing a protective shield to ward off offensive mental, physical, and spiritual attacks. June can catch us with our guard down as we are taken in by the beauty of this month. Therefore, revitalize actions with inner meaning, lest you burn out and succumb to harmful lower frequencies!

Contemplate the Summer Season

The new moon beckons us to reflect and be insightful. The summer climate brings some of us visions of warm-weather activities and fun in the sun! What do you think about summer, and what does it mean to you? Draw a picture, cut one out from a magazine (if you still buy them), or print one out from the Internet. Do you have a special scene in your mind that reminds you of summer? Illustrate it. Compare your summer reflection to that of other seasons.

Review Old Decisions

We've all had to make tough decisions in life—either between two good choices or two bad ones. While you don't want to beat yourself up over past choices, sometimes it's a good thing to review what went right, what went wrong, and what you might do differently next time.

Think about a time when you had a difficult decision to make. Ask yourself what might have happened if you had chosen a different path:

• What would be different in your life?

_____

_____

_____

_____

_____

• Would things be better or worse? What would you have lost by trading outcomes?

_____

_____

_____

_____

_____

• When faced with a tough choice in the future, how will you decide?

_____

_____

_____

_____

_____

Most importantly, your answers will help you move past difficult times and define your priorities so that you can feel good about where you are now and where you're headed in the future.

We are going to the moon—that is not very far. Man has so much farther to go within himself.

—Anaïs Nin, author

Protect Yourself from Negative Psychic Influences

Unfortunately, we all find ourselves in situations filled with negative or toxic energy once in a while. Here are three ways to protect yourself in those scenarios:

- Visualize yourself encased in a bubble of white light, surrounded head to toe and front to back.

- Wear a piece of black obsidian or carry it in your pocket or purse. It absorbs stress-related psychic aggression emanating from other people. The vibration of this stone promotes protection.

- Stop negative energy that's coming your way by "throwing energy." Simply lift a few fingers on each hand for a second and push energy away toward your left and right. (Of course, when driving, keep your hands on the steering wheel. Dispel negative energy when you get to a red light.)

Decorate a Candle for a Friend

The waxing moon phase is centered on giving and expanding, so it's a lovely time to make a handcrafted gift for a friend. Imagine what a special friend would want. Let the frequency of the waxing moon be an inspiration to be a giver.

You will need: a white pillar candle and decorations to add to it

1. Engrave or decorate a white pillar candle with things that a friend could appreciate and relate to. (The candle is more of a decoration than something to light, but if you put the ornaments low enough, the candle could be lit for a short time.) For example:

    - Glue a button on the candle if your friend sews.

    - Paste a guitar picture or drawing if they play.

    - Attach a heart made out of felt if they are looking for love.

2. When you present it, tell your friend to light it for at least a few seconds or minutes and visualize these things coming their way.

Write Your Own Affirmations

As the moon comes into its full glory and power, your energy is increasing as well. Before you hit your full stride during the full moon, focus your energy so that you can achieve one or two specific goals this month. Writing an affirmation can help you pinpoint where you want to direct your attention during this time.

For example, you might write: *During the full moon this month, I intend to [insert your own goal here]. I will achieve this by [add actions that will help you reach your goal]. I am confident that I can complete [your goal] by working with the moon's energy.*

Try writing your own affirmations— and adjust them to each moon cycle!

Create Your Own Symbols

This lunar phase is all about creating and producing. For this exercise, draw as many symbols as you can that connote love, peace, going green, balance, and positivity. Be sure to capture elements related to your body, mind, and spirit. You can use these symbols at a later date for candle magic, crafts, writing notes, or even frosting cupcakes! Look around you (without going to the Internet) and find symbols that remind you of all things good. Is it a bird or the yin and yang symbol? Draw all over the page like a collage. Add more later at your leisure.

Avoid Absorbing Toxic Energy

When you encounter another person who seems like they are surrounded by lots of negative vibes, clear your body of their energy when they leave your presence. You can do this anytime at any moon phase. But when the moon is waxing, people seem to be a bit higher strung, and you may find yourself doing this more frequently at this particular phase. It's an easy process: Simply take your hands and shake them at your sides. You are shaking the toxic vibration away from you, like dust. The other person may not have meant you any harm, but you don't want to be left with that residue. Write down some situations or names of people that often leave you feeling drained of positive energy.

Track Your Full Moon Mood

The vibrational energy of the full moon affects everyone in different ways. Why not track your moods during full moons to see what it does to you? Check the circles that apply to you on this full moon. You'll do this exercise during each full moon to see if your mood stays the same or changes. *This full moon, I feel:*

○ Adventurous	○ Healthy	○ Magical
○ Anxious	○ Hopeful	○ Sexy
○ Athletic	○ Intuitive	○ So-So
○ Attractive	○ In love	○ Theatrical
○ Bored	○ In lust	○ Tired
○ Depressed	○ Jealous	○ Worried
○ Empowered	○ Lonely	○ _____
○ Generous	○ Lost	○ _____

Create Your Own Full Moon Talisman

A talisman is an object that protects you, and during a full moon (which encourages creativity and intuition) is a great time to make one. Follow these steps:

You will need: a chain or cord, a charm or medallion of some sort that can get wet, and some salt

1. Wash your charm or medallion in cold water under your faucet and visualize negative energy going down the drain with the water. Now it's clear of any residual energy that may have been on it. Dry it off.

2. Place the charm outside in full view of the moon. If that is not possible, put it near a window or door that gets moonlight. No window? Draw a full moon and place the charm under that. The moon will eventually pass over the area, so it doesn't have to be in a perfect spot. Throw a bit of salt on it and say:

   "This was once an ordinary charm.

   Now keep me safe from fear and harm.

   And so it is."

3. Leave it in place for twelve hours (if possible), then remove the salt and clean it a bit. Hang the charm on the chain or cord, and wear your powerful talisman whenever you feel the need for protection.

Seek Extra Strength for Forgiveness

The full moon is a time when emotions, intuition, and passions are at their peak. Although we think of letting go and forgiving during a waning moon, sometimes we struggle to do that in particularly difficult situations. In those cases, you can call on the energy of the full moon to lend a hand for pushing emotional traps out of your mind and spirit. Absolution needs a lot of guts and strength—let the heightened energy of the full moon provide that extra boost.

If you are bothered by a past event that sticks in your mind like glue, try this exercise to sort things out:

1. Write down something that happened and the name of the person involved.

2. Jot down reasons why forgiveness has been particularly difficult.

3. In a positive, nonvengeful way, imagine what you want to happen that could bring you closer (or all the way) to total forgiveness. Write it down.

Don't let someone or something from your past ruin your future. You are stronger than that.

Let Go of Social Media Bullies' Influence

We think that when we leave adolescence behind and enter the adult world, we won't have to deal with mean people or bullies anymore. How wrong we are! Unfortunately, the Internet makes it all too easy for people to type insults and comments that they would never in a million years say to someone in person. If you've been hurt by cyberbullying, the waning moon is a good time to let go of the pain and shame that's often associated with any kind of harassment.

Here's a little ritual that will help you release those distressing emotions:

1. Light a candle. As you hold your flame to the wick, visualize your raw emotions making that flame burn bright.

2. Recite a simple incantation to yourself, like, "I will not allow myself to feel humiliated by a cruel person's words. Their words are not truth. My reality is truth. I release my painful emotions now."

3. Blow out the flame, and visualize your painful emotions dissipating in the smoke.

And remember, when someone is unkind for no reason, it says far more about them than it does about you.

Get Over a Bad Relationship

The waning moon, with its power of depleting unwanted things, is the best time to get over a relationship. Try this ritual to help release your relationship. Follow these steps:

You will need: one black candle, a container for your candle, and matches or a lighter

1. Envision a circle of white light around you and the entire area in which you are sitting. (This serves as a form of protection from negative forces.)

2. Light your candle and repeat the following words three times: "Dear [person's name], our past is through, I wish the best for me and you. And so it is, we both are free, our time is done, so blessed be!"

3. Extinguish the candle and throw it away or bury it. Write down how you feel before and after the ritual.

Shower Your Negative Vibes Away

Showering isn't only for cleansing the body; it can cleanse your mind and spirit as well! When you are filled with negativity, send that mind clutter down the drain. It's freeing in your mind to "see" the old clear out and have a fresh start. The waning moon does the same thing: Light wanes and wanes until it jump-starts with some replacement energy. As you shower, picture your body encompassed by gray light. As the water washes over you, that light gets brighter and brighter until you are surrounded in a bright white glow. (For a quicker fix, you can also wash your hands and do the same thing.)

Remind Yourself How You've Overcome Past Challenges

When you're faced with challenging situations and painful emotions, sometimes it's helpful to think back on other difficult times in order to remind yourself that you're pretty darned strong and resilient. Ask yourself:

• What was the most difficult thing I've had to overcome?

_____
_____
_____
_____
_____

• How did I feel when this first happened? Did I believe I would get through it, or was there a time when I thought I would never survive it?

_____
_____
_____
_____
_____

- How did I deal with it?

_____
_____
_____
_____

- Were there things I could have done better or differently?

_____
_____
_____
_____

- When did the situation begin to improve?

_____
_____
_____
_____

- How did I let go of the most painful part of the situation and move forward?

_____
_____
_____
_____

The waning moon helps you lay the groundwork for renewal, so don't get pulled down into sadness or negativity during this exercise—instead, focus on your strengths!

The moon will guide you through the night with her brightness, but she will always dwell in the darkness, in order to be seen.

—Shannon L. Alder, author

July

Embrace Positivity

I love a summer thunderstorm, so in that spirit, think of July as a time of letting built-up creative energy loose. Thunderclouds build. Electrically charged expanding air discharges as a snap of lightning, illuminating the sky. Thunderclaps resound. A downpour of rejuvenating, cooling rain quenches the earth. The air is clean, ionic balance has been restored, and the soil is enriched. After a thunderstorm, the world is a rainbow, bright and full of promise. Once the storm has passed, clarity and vibrancy, along with new untapped powers, can emerge, and new successes can be attained.

To honor this moon cycle, step into your authentic self and step up your expressive powers. Trust in the magic of your own creative power. Let go of anything that holds you back; break any chains of confinement. Let your energy flow in ways that electrify and light up your life. Make a joyful noise that commands attention. Bask in the silver lining of dark clouds and soak up the positive, regenerative energy.

Track Your Spiritual Self

Your spiritual side deserves self-realization and growth, just like your physical and mental sides. But what are you really doing to promote your spiritual well-being? Whether you are religious or nondenominational spiritual, you should have some type of plan. Creating that plan is in itself a positive exercise, because it helps you, other people, and the planet. If you don't have a plan yet, this is a good time to create one, when the new moon phase promotes contemplation and reflection.

Do you plan on praying more, meditating more, or volunteering for those in need? Are you going to contribute financially? What will move you further along your spiritual path? Record your thoughts and ideas here. Go back to this page in a month and read this entry and see if you have achieved or improved your spiritual journey.

Try a Spell Comparison

Find your favorite spell or make one up. Then do the same spell in different ways, write down the differences, and note which one you feel was more effective or stronger. Here are some examples of how to do spells differently: If doing a money spell, use all white candles in one spell and two green and one white in another. Use different incense, gemstones, locations, and incantations or chants. Consider facing in a different direction. The moon is new, so think up new spell variations! Get out of your old spell routine and start coming up with alternative approaches.

Focus On Happiness

This new moon lifts mood, raises energy, boosts confidence, and imbues resilience for recovering from setbacks. Select something that induces happiness, be it sports, people, places, foods—whatever fills you with joy. Write a brief description of the sensations you experience when engaged with whatever it is you enjoy.

For example, one of my favorite activities is sailing, so I might write:

…the boundless sense of freedom and potential to explore what lies over the horizon.

…the rhythmic rocking movement of the waves.

…the strong connection to nature.

…the sun-warmed breeze and fresh sea air on my face.

…when the wind fills the sails, the boat picks up speed, lists, and comes to life.

Define Your Perfect Day

The moon increases her light as it heads toward a perfect full moon. You too can head toward full-moon flawlessness. For this exercise, explore and shape new possibilities in your mind by imagining, designing, and describing in detail your perfect day. You choose if you want to make it an "attainable" or a "dream" day.

List the elements you consider essential to a perfect day. Make a schedule that maps out your itinerary, from the moment you wake up until you close your eyes to sleep. Then flesh it out with specifics. Where are you? Who are you with? What are you doing? How do you feel? Later, pick one of the parts of your day and work it into your life sometime in the coming week.

Celebrate Your Life

There is always much to celebrate, even in the small, quiet moments. When we take the time to notice, move out of routine, and observe with an eye toward veneration, we bolster our well-being and mitigate stress. Commit to loving yourself and celebrating who you are and all that you do. Start by journaling about:

• The unique talents, abilities, and skills you bring to life.

_____

_____

_____

_____

• What you like about your life and what's working.

_____

_____

_____

_____

• Ways you're realizing your purpose.

_____

_____

_____

_____

• What makes you a rare, valuable, one-of-a-kind keeper.

_____

_____

_____

_____

When done, honor the essence that is you with a commemorative act. Say a blessing; dance around; sing a song; light a candle; toast or treat yourself with a healthy physical reward. After all, you're something wonderful and so worth celebrating.

The moon is the friendliest of the celestial bodies, after all, glowing warm and white and welcoming.

—Seanan McGuire, author, Down Among the Sticks and Bones

Visualize the Happiest Day of Your Life

To reconnect with the joy and beauty of your life, meditate on and then journal about all the details of the happiest day of your life.

1. Clear your mind and take several deep breaths.

2. Now immerse yourself in the reality of that day. Recreate the environment as best you can, and really try to feel, hear, see, touch, and taste any relevant setting, people, animals, plants, weather, colors, smells, sounds, flavors, and textures you experienced.

3. Remember and explore additional feelings (other than happiness) that come up.

4. Take several more deep breaths and reflect on why this was a wonderful day for you. Write down any feelings you experienced and any gratitude you have for that day and its events. Notice if this opens your awareness and connects you to happiness in the present moment as well.

Make a Desire Pouch

Investing time and energy in crafting a desire pouch is a powerful activity for channeling positivity and creativity during this phase of the moon.

You will need: a pouch (or fabric, thread, ribbon, or string to make one) and symbolic items

1. Set your intention, concentrating your focus on your goal.

2. Give thought and attention to your design. It can be simple or elaborate. Decide what material and color your pouch should be. It should represent the desired outcome and evoke potent associations. You can purchase a pouch or make one out of a fabric scrap.

3. Gather corresponding symbolic objects that signify, resonate with, or are important to the outcome—affirmations, quotes, charms, coins, beads, buttons, tokens, jewelry, pictures, seeds, feathers, herbs/spices, leaves, and stones or crystals.

4. Clear your mind and place the items in the pouch while visualizing your desire. Give thanks and positive vibes to your endeavor.

5. Seal the pouch with thread, ribbon, string, or yarn. Keep it wherever you choose.

Journal about Your Downtime

We all need balance in our lives; this includes a break from obligations. Downtime clears the mind; allows for processing and recovery; and re-energizes us. Downtime isn't being lazy; it's important for maintaining optimal mental, emotional, physical, and spiritual health. You should never feel bad when you need a break to recharge, because unencumbered free time has proven to promote increased productivity and creativity. Journal about what you would do with one day a week free from any obligation. Make that day a reality once in a while.

Track Your Full Moon Mood

The vibrational energy of the full moon affects everyone in different ways. Why not track your moods during full moons to see what it does to you? Check the circles that apply to you on this full moon. You'll do this exercise during each full moon to see if your mood stays the same or changes. *This full moon, I feel:*

○ Adventurous	○ Healthy	○ Magical
○ Anxious	○ Hopeful	○ Sexy
○ Athletic	○ Intuitive	○ So-So
○ Attractive	○ In love	○ Theatrical
○ Bored	○ In lust	○ Tired
○ Depressed	○ Jealous	○ Worried
○ Empowered	○ Lonely	○ _____
○ Generous	○ Lost	○ _____

Give Yourself
Advice

It's time to get in touch with your lunar self this full moon, when the celestial orb is bursting with brilliance and pours down insights like rain. It's time to share some wisdom—with yourself.

If you came from the future and talked to yourself when you were growing up, what would you advise yourself? Think in terms of creativity, well-being, and self-worth. Would you tell yourself to not take that art class because you are only trying painting to impress some other person? Or would you tell yourself to continue to write poetry even though publishers don't have much interest, because your poems help you express yourself in a healthy way? How about telling yourself to buy a particular stock or not to eat too much bacon? Write anything and everything you would like yourself to know. Use these thoughts to inform your future plans.

Ask for World Peace

This ritual is an appeal to the universe to envelop the planet in love and serenity.

You will need: jasmine aroma in some form (incense, fresh flowers, oil, or a scented candle), several candles in any shade of blue, and matches

1. Release the jasmine aroma around your work area (light the incense, scatter fresh flowers around the room, diffuse the oil, etc.). Arrange the blue candles to make a small circle in front of you.

2. Light the candles.

3. As you light each one, say, "Our planet is sacred; we will have peace."

Liberate Yourself from Fears with Citrine

To merge the positive vibe of July and the occurrence of the waning moon, free yourself from your stresses. Do you struggle with anxiety or stress? If so, write down what is bothering you. To aid you in resolving this situation, try wearing or meditating with citrine. Citrine is a yellowish crystal that has many healing properties, one of which is that it helps calm fears and rid you of anxiety. Citrine is easily found in forms of jewelry. (Remember to clear any gemstone after you purchase it. One simple way is to run cold water over it and visualize any former energy going down the drain.) When you wear citrine during the waning moon, its vibration assists you in discharging emotions of distress. It's best to wear it, or you can carry it in a pocket, purse, or wallet.

Say No

When you don't know how to say no to others, and you say yes to avoid a conflict or keep people from thinking badly of you, you bring yourself down.

Sometimes when you do what is best for you, it ends up being what is best for all. Maybe someone asked you to go somewhere, and though you didn't want to go, you said yes. Then you found out they only asked you in the first place out of obligation. Use the space on this page to imagine scenarios in which you'll be better off saying no. Fill in the blank.

The next time I…

 # Cope with Loss in a Positive Way

Rituals are symbolic behaviors we perform related to meaningful and challenging life events and the emotions surrounding them. In this releasing phase of the waning moon, take some time to think about, identify, examine, and journal about a familiar ritual, ceremony, or rite related to coping with loss. This could be a simple, mundane loss (like a tennis match) or a more complex, life-changing one (death of a loved one).

Which ritual do you feel compelled to do? What does this ritual mean or symbolize for you? How does enacting it impact your feelings? What do you enjoy about it? Does this ritual foster a sense of peace and/or connection? Is there anything about it you dislike or would like to improve?

Learn from Last Month

Release a few things from the last month, as the waning moon releases its energy slowly—but remember what you learned.

• What wellness issue is going away or have you thought about freeing yourself from?

_____

_____

_____

_____

_____

• Is there anything last month you thought was a challenge and now you can laugh about it?

_____

_____

_____

_____

_____

• What was the worst thing you ate, or a restaurant you visited that you would not try again?

_____

_____

_____

_____

• Was there a time when you saw, texted, or talked to a particular person, and you're glad that's over?

_____

_____

_____

_____

_____

• Generally, what about last month are you glad to get rid of?

_____

_____

_____

_____

_____

The moon is...always there, watching, steadfast, knowing us in our light and dark moments, changing forever just as we do. Every day it's a different version of itself.

—Tahereh Mafi, author, Shatter Me

August

Get Romantic

While Earth's fruitful bounty overflows with plenty of fresh produce this month, the August moon likewise gushes with emotional abundance, especially the miraculous healing power of love. This hot August moon cycle is a great time to squeeze out the last zest of summer before the cooler days ahead. Take some time to live in the radiant love that permeates and illuminates every aspect of life, including your love of self and love of others.

Love is opening, welcoming, and accepting. It takes you into unknown territory, expands your horizons, and raises your vibrational frequency. Romancing that which you love requires your full attention, forethought, imagination, and great care. Summer can afford you the time to fully embody and express the true depth of affection and appreciation you have for your loved ones.

Think about Good Memories with Your Partner

Whether you're in a new relationship or you've been with your mate for decades, the new moon is a good time to take stock of the positive aspects of your love connection. Think about the things that you may take for granted in your partner: Do they work hard for the family? Are they a wonderful caretaker when you're not feeling well? Do the two of you laugh so hard that your sides hurt? Whatever it is that you appreciate about your relationship, write it down here…and then tell your partner how grateful you are for them!

Assess Whether They're The One

Have you met someone new recently? Wondering if they are The One, or just The Current One? It can be difficult to know whether your excitement over a new partner is because this person is fantastic, or because the relationship is brand-new. Ask yourself:

• What's the best thing about this person?

_____

_____

_____

_____

• Is this person respectful of my beliefs?

_____

_____

_____

_____

• Why do I like spending time with this person?

_____

_____

_____

_____

• Do my friends think this person is good for me?

_____

_____

_____

_____

• When I'm not with this person, how do I feel?

_____

_____

_____

_____

The new moon can give you the clarity to assess a relationship for what it is. The most important thing is that you don't try to force a connection with someone. If it's meant to be, it will be!

Write Down Four Things You Want in a Relationship

Long-term relationships tend to lapse into comfort and repetition—not that these are bad things, but we often forget that love is something we need to nurture. The new moon provides just the right energy for you to step back and think about what you can improve in your relationships throughout the coming month. Try to think of an idea for each of the coming phases. Consider the energy that each phase brings, and try to match your actions to that energy. (For example, the waxing moon is a time to focus on increasing things, so this could be a time to try to spend more time with your mate.)

New moon:

_____

_____

_____

_____

Waxing moon:

_____

_____

_____

_____

Full moon:

_____

_____

_____

_____

Waning moon:

_____

_____

_____

_____

Write a Love Poem

One of the best gifts you can give a loved one is a piece of writing that comes from your heart and soul. During the waxing moon, when you're focused on bringing more of what you want into your reality, think about writing a love poem for your partner. I know some of you will say, "I'm not a writer. I could never express myself like that!" Well, you'll never know until you try.

First, sit in a quiet space and think about the things you love and appreciate about your mate. Is it the way they care for you, or the little things they do without thinking? How does your relationship make you feel? Safe? Invincible? Give it some thought, and then jot down key words and phrases. Those can become the foundation for your poem.

I've never seen a moon in the sky that, if it didn't take my breath away, at least misplaced it for a moment.

—Colin Farrell, actor

Play Eight
Questions with Your Partner

The spirit of the waxing moon should encourage you to grow your relationship with your partner. This is a fun little exercise you can repeat every August to see how your relationship has evolved. You and your partner should answer these separately, then compare your thoughts.

1. What is the most unique thing about your partner?

2. If your partner could save one thing in a fire (besides you), what would it be?

3. What song reminds you of your partner? Why?

4. How does your partner react to a traffic jam?

5. Would your partner choose a home in the city or country?

6. What is your partner's dream job?

7. Would your partner rather stay in or go out on a Friday night?

8. Where would your partner travel to if money were no object?

Practice Candle Magic to Attract Love

Because the waxing moon helps to bring things into our lives, it's a good time to cast a spell for that perfect partner if you're single.

You will need: a white candle, a toothpick (or something else with which to engrave your candle), and matches

1. First, sit quietly and think about the kind of person you'd like for a mate. Don't focus on any one person in particular; rather, use the following lines to list the characteristics of your perfect partner. You can include physical traits, but try to focus more on personality and how this person lives life. (That's because if the perfect person comes in a physical package that's a little shorter than what you imagined, most people would be okay with that!)

_____

_____

_____

_____

_____

_____

2. Somewhere on the candle, engrave your initials and a question mark, which will represent the person who will be coming into your life.

3. Now light a white candle and cast your spell, reciting something along these lines: "I light this candle under the waxing moon so that I might bring my true love into my life. I ask the moon to make this person visible to me. So mote it be." Add your own embellishments to this spell to make it your own.

The moon puts on an elegant show, different every time in shape, colour and nuance.

—Arthur Smith, comedian

Make a Memory

If you are in a meaningful relationship that's developing more each day (like the waxing moon!), frame a memory. August moon names (like Corn Moon or Grain Moon) are all about gathering, and in this exercise, you'll gather and celebrate a memory.

You will need: a picture frame and pens or markers

1. On the lines, write down how you and your partner first met, or a loving memory you two share. You can embellish your words with rose petals, hearts, or a picture if you like.

2. Next, glue the memory on to the cardboard that comes with a picture frame (or make one to fit).

3. Give it to your partner when the August moon is full.

Track Your Full Moon Mood

The vibrational energy of the full moon affects everyone in different ways. Why not track your moods during full moons to see what it does to you? Check the circles that apply to you on this full moon. You'll do this exercise during each full moon to see if your mood stays the same or changes. *This full moon, I feel:*

○ Adventurous	○ Healthy	○ Magical
○ Anxious	○ Hopeful	○ Sexy
○ Athletic	○ Intuitive	○ So-So
○ Attractive	○ In love	○ Theatrical
○ Bored	○ In lust	○ Tired
○ Depressed	○ Jealous	○ Worried
○ Empowered	○ Lonely	○ _____
○ Generous	○ Lost	○ _____

Embrace the Power of Pyramids to Improve Your Sex Life

It's said that a pyramid built to the same proportions as the Great Cheops Pyramid (more commonly called Giza) in Egypt can produce so much energy that it can preserve food, cure headaches, and activate sexual urges. Those are only a few of the influences it has! Combine this shape with the energetic force of the full moon, and it's like a double sexual whammy.

During this moon phase, invest in a small copper pyramid, which will run you about $15. Why copper? Copper is a conductor of electricity and can amplify the movement of energy around us. It is used to conduct positive energy into the area in which it is placed. Put your pyramid under your bed or at the foot of your bed. Document your romantic encounters with and without the pyramid.

Reinvent Yourself for a Day

Relive a Romantic Memory

The full moon exerts its power on all of us in unexpected ways. You may feel more energetic, your moods may shift unexpectedly, or you may get some of your best ideas during this time. If you've been feeling like you need to change things up in your life—try a new haircut, for example, or buy an outfit that's a little trendier than how you usually dress—this is the time! If you're single, this is a good time to get on a dating website or to finally agree to go out on the town with your friends. The full moon is a time for action, so go get your dreams!

Sometimes the best way to bring new love into your life is to make sure you're letting go of old loves and patterns. The waning period of the moon is about release and reflection, so the lunar timing is very suitable. One way to let go is to revisit the past in an effort to put it to rest. Think about the most romantic thing you've ever experienced, and ask yourself these questions:

- Who was the person? How would you describe them?

_____

_____

_____

_____

- Why did the relationship end?

_____

_____

_____

_____

- How can you let go of any regrets associated with those memories and take that energy into a new relationship?

_____

_____

_____

_____

Let Bad Habits Sail Away

When you live day in and day out with someone, it's sometimes difficult to overlook their less favorable (or downright annoying) habits. One nice thing you can do during this phase of the moon is to have a kindhearted chat with your partner about his or her behavior, and then make a paper sailboat to represent this habit and let it set sail. (If you don't live near a lake or ocean, just sail it in the bathtub.) While you watch your paper vessel, say, "From this time on, this habit be gone. And so it is."

It will eventually sink, which is just the symbolism you and your partner want—the behavior is going, and along with it, your resentment. (And remember that turnabout is fair play—send some of your own less-than-ideal habits sailing too!) Journal about the experience.

Replace Unhealthy Habits
with Healing Activities

You and your partner can focus on releasing unhealthy habits during the waning moon. Together, make a list of things you'd like to change. They might include:

- Smoking
- Drinking
- Overeating
- Not exercising
- High stress levels
- Anger and/or fighting

    Depending on what the issue is, develop a plan to end the toxic behaviors and replace them with something else. For example, if the two of you are highly stressed, try a meditation practice together. If overeating is the problem, make a date to clean out your pantry and toss the cookies and chips. If your relationship is on the rocks, think about couples counseling to release the tension between you.

        Unhealthy Habit   ⟶   Healing Activity

Turn the Tables

Here's a fun little game for you and your partner: Switch roles and show the other person how you perceive their behaviors. Keep it light, and portray their good characteristics as well as their not-so-good traits. This isn't meant to be a mocking exercise; rather, it should open up a dialogue about what you most love about each other as well as what the two of you could be doing better. Some suggestions:

- Set up a specific situation, like driving in the car together.

- Have a time limit—no more than five minutes.

- Take note of what you like about "your" behavior and what you don't.

- And finally…discuss!

Start positive and end on a positive note. Briefly talk about what you have learned and how it has helped you understand the other person. A hug at the end is always a good idea. Jot down some things you learned about yourself during this activity.

September

Strengthen Your Body, Mind, and Spirit Connection

With the autumn equinox being a prominent celestial event, this is a month charged with balanced solar and lunar energies. As we let go of the light of summer and turn toward an inner flame, we can take stock of our physical, mental, and spiritual energy for navigating the coming darker winter months.

Often a hurried time of returning to busy school schedules and readying our homes and bodies for winter, this moon can inspire a quiet, contemplative time. In a moment of solitude, we may ponder what we've sown, tended to, and harvested earlier this year. Have our ideas and goals received the care and attention they needed to bear fruit?

This is an excellent time for pondering various aspects of your life and investing some time considering what areas of your life need balance. What areas are flourishing? Which are lacking? What debts need to be settled? How can the light and shadow aspects become more equal? Try to achieve that yin and yang steadiness.

Contemplate the Fall Season

The new moon is small but mighty, so let it shine in your imagination and creative self. Think about what fall means to you, and write it down or draw a representation of it. Consider drawing a tree (found in any region) that represents this season, maybe surrounded by freshly fallen leaves and autumn colors. Compare your thoughts to those for other seasons.

Journal Your Workout Routine

Try Three New Foods

Examining your exercise routine through journaling offers valuable, often profound benefits, impacting not only your workout and writing, but also your perspective on life. Are you more comfortable exercising or less so during the new moon? Is it a good time for a quiet practice such as yoga (thanks to the calm energy), or do you feel it's a better time to rest the body and not do yoga at all? Notice, reflect on, and journal about lessons learned from your fitness practice that have expanded understanding in other areas of your life. If you need inspiration, think about your answers to these questions:

- What fitness or exercise skills have you learned that deepened or enriched your appreciation for life?

- How has your practice helped you become more connected not just to your own body and mind, but to a larger community or a larger consciousness?

What are some healthy new foods you'd like to try this month, when that new moon is nudging you toward new undertakings? Make a list of at least three foods you would like to incorporate into your eating habits. Write down recipes, takeout places, grocery stores, and restaurants so you have specific ideas to go along with the food. (Don't forget farmers' markets and local food sourcing when possible.) The next time you're hungry, go to your list and try something you've never had or somewhere you have never visited.

1.

2.

3.

Try Moon Bathing

All life on Earth evolved and continues to develop in an environment regulated by solar and lunar cycles. Moon bathing (simply exposing your skin to the moon) is one mindful way to access the moon's light. Environmental cues from moonlight can impact a variety of aspects of your body—including powerful endocrine hormones, mood-boosting endorphins, vitamin D, and nitric oxide—which affect fertility, sleep cycles, and stress levels. The only way to absorb these unique benefits is to spend time outside on moonlit nights.

During this energy-building, powerhouse phase, take advantage of this gift from nature. Take a walk—or even better, dance—in the refreshing, ethereal light of the moon. Observe, connect with, and breathe in the radiance, allowing the pure and serene energy to enter your body. Be sure to expose some of your skin to the light for at least thirty minutes. Write about what you sense. Did you feel the power?

Show Gratitude
for Wildlife

Research has finally proven what many of us have always inherently known—climbing a tree, collecting shells along the beach, gardening, bird watching, or playing with a companion animal invokes joy, reduces stress, and bolsters overall well-being. Scientific studies show that healthy immersion in a natural environment decreases stress hormones, boosts energy levels, promotes positive emotions, and increases immune system function. The amplified light of the moon can bring our attention to animals we don't normally see.

During this moon phase, engage with nature to experience the beauty of the wild and the flora and fauna that inhabit it. If you feel moved, start up a conversation with a tree, a plant, or an animal you encounter. Listen, and record your impressions. Before you return to the human realm, take a moment to express your admiration, respect, and thanks for the wild things.

Write Down What You Succeeded at Today

It's vital for morale to recognize and praise progress on a daily basis. The compounding moon glow and the vibration of her energy is always prompting you to remember your successes. During this moon phase, review and list as many successes as you can from your day. Your triumphs may be small (you got out of bed!) or momentous (you got a promotion). What's important is to acknowledge them and ready your mind to welcome more success into your life.

1.

2.

3.

4.

5.

Expand Your Spiritual Habits

Ideally, you should be caring for, nourishing, and developing all aspects of your being (whether physical, emotional, intellectual, or spiritual) to maintain wellness and encourage growth. The waxing phase, with its shaft of what appears to be expanding light, can lend a hand to help activate your nonphysical self. To tend to your spiritual essence, explore practices that will help you stay connected. Try one of these activities and journal about your experience.

• Fit five to twenty minutes of meditation into your day.

• Take a temporary vow of silence; reflect on and analyze recurring life patterns and look for deeper meanings.

_____

_____

_____

_____

• Eliminate negativity and walk on the bright side; vow to view your life more positively and reframe your thinking on select situations.

• Ask yourself: When do I feel most connected to life? Where do I seek spiritual sustenance?

_____

_____

_____

_____

_____

• Ponder your purpose by asking: Who am I? What is my purpose? What do I value most? What is the biggest unanswered question in my life?

_____

_____

_____

_____

_____

Everybody has a little bit of the sun and moon in them.... Everyone is part of a connected cosmic system.

—Suzy Kassem, author, "Part Sun and Moon"

Track Your Full Moon Mood

The vibrational energy of the full moon affects everyone in different ways. Why not track your moods during full moons to see what it does to you? Check the circles that apply to you on this full moon. You'll do this exercise during each full moon to see if your mood stays the same or changes. *This full moon, I feel:*

○ Adventurous	○ Healthy	○ Magical
○ Anxious	○ Hopeful	○ Sexy
○ Athletic	○ Intuitive	○ So-So
○ Attractive	○ In love	○ Theatrical
○ Bored	○ In lust	○ Tired
○ Depressed	○ Jealous	○ Worried
○ Empowered	○ Lonely	○ _____
○ Generous	○ Lost	○ _____

_____

_____

_____

_____

_____

_____

_____

_____

_____

_____

Create a Full Moon Mind Map

Mind maps are visual tools created to represent, organize, enlighten, and make creative connections around a central topic. You can use them to brainstorm novel ideas, show relationships, design things, devise approaches, and solve problems. The process taps into both the imaginative right brain and logical left brain hemispheres to construct and produce an image-rich, network-like map of associations. The mystic light of the full moon, which radiates inventiveness, will assist you in your map-making process. Here's what to do, either in the space here or on a separate piece of paper:

1. Write your idea in the center of an unlined page (ideally landscape-oriented). Circle it. Add color, shape, imagery, drawings, or photos as needed to inspire yourself.

2. Think of links and ideas related to the main topic. Write down any thoughts that pop up using keywords or images. Don't judge or organize; just write!

3. Now add lines, branches, arrows, and other symbols to connect the main idea to the related ideas around the page.

4. If needed, rewrite key ideas on a clean sheet in order to organize your mind mapping in a meaningful way.

Write
Thank-You Cards

Even in these digital days, when it's relatively easy to stay connected, people still come and go, passing through our lives, never to be seen or talked to again. We often don't fully comprehend how much those people have shaped our lives and who we are as a result of our interaction.

It's both empowering and freeing to write gratitude notes to people who have significantly impacted your life but who you never properly thanked—either because you initially weren't aware of the scope of influence or you haven't availed yourself of the opportunity.

Whether or not you'll send these letters, take the time now to remember and express your appreciation in writing for whatever you experienced or learned from someone who positively contributed to where you are today. The full moon has a way of sending out a frequency that may somehow touch those who we wish to thank. And sending out that kind of energy is so gratifying.

Explore the Differences Between Alone Time and Loneliness

There's a difference between having alone time and being lonely. Finding alone time can be key if you share living space with a roommate(s) or family members. When is the last time you had alone time? How did you feel? What did you do?

Now think about a time that you felt lonely, whether in the short or long term. What did you do to combat it? Did you keep your radio or television on for company? Did you sign up for a dating app? Think about how you let go of the loneliness or how you enjoyed others letting go of you for a short while and giving you space.

Allow the words to let loose onto this page just as the waning moon is releasing that energy it gathered after the full moon.

Purify Your Home

Your home may be clean…but its energy could be a dust bowl! The moon is waning and demands liberation. So set the metaphorical dust bunnies free to be recycled into particles of positive blessings that rearrange themselves as love and safety.

This ceremony can be done anywhere you call home, even a single room.

You will need: one black candle (any size, shape, or scent) and matches or a lighter

1. Put the candle anywhere your intuition tells you is a good location. Light the candle and say:

   "Candlelight clear

   Energy flow

   To up above, from here below.

   The moon she wanes and that's the key;

   Bless this place and blessed be."

2. Concentrate on the candlelight. Visualize low-frequency or dark energy going up into the cosmos with the smoke.

3. Completely extinguish the flame. Throw out or bury the candle. Any negative energy is gone!

Compose a Rite of Passage

A rite of passage is a ceremony marking a milestone when a person transitions from one phase of life to another. Nearly all societies recognize and honor key moments with ritual events. These are powerful, because they help both the individual and the society shift their perception to recognize new states of being.

To design a personal rite of passage, meditate on and conceptualize a journey that connects with and symbolizes something meaningful. This could be an accomplishment to celebrate, a painful event to be confronted, or a challenge to be overcome. Immerse yourself in the feelings surrounding this change and imagine what the future will look like.

You will need: items that remind you of your specific event, or use these general items: a bell to ring out negativity, a purple candle for wisdom, and matches

1. Ring the bell three times, light the candle, then say, "I pass through this gate to my new stage of life."

2. Take a step forward to symbolize your movement into a new phase.

As you move into a new phase, like the waning moon is moving into a lesser light, reflect on and journal about your experience.

October

Free Your Inner Desires

As the earth's energy winds down, exhausted from high levels of summer activity and continual production, we move further into a time of decrease, dormancy, and darkness. The moon presides over crisp and clear nights and imparts energy for change. Just as the trees shed their leaves, it's an appropriate time to let go of and mourn that which is past, gone, and no longer serves our highest and best interests.

As our shadow side moves forward, hidden aspects of our being are unearthed. Inner desires are unveiled; karma is fulfilled. Use this moon cycle energy of dissolution and decomposition for inner cleansing. Separate yourself from harmful substances, relationships, habits, and situations. Experience and then free yourself from darker emotions of anger, sadness, and bitterness so they cannot fester and cause disharmony or dis-ease. Remember ancestors who have lived before us and honor them.

Reduce Stress with a Spiced Citrus Pomander

The new moon phase brings forth individuality and novel ideas. So aim for being creative and seasonal with this exercise. Orange oil, known for its warm, uplifting scent, has recently been credited with reducing fear and stress associated with post-traumatic stress disorder by research conducted at George Washington University. To preserve the refreshing essence and its stress-relieving benefits, creatively decorate an orange with cloves to make a pomander.

You will need: a few oranges, some whole cloves, and a tool to puncture the oranges (oranges and tangerines are fun to make near Halloween because of their color; other citrus fruit such as lemons, limes, kumquats, and grapefruits work as well, though)

1. Use wooden skewers or nails to punch holes in the orange skin, and insert the whole cloves into the holes.

2. Each day for a couple of weeks, roll the oranges in a blend of equal parts cinnamon, nutmeg, and cloves with a pinch of orris root powder. The oranges will gradually desiccate and become lightweight.

3. Once dried, they make lovely lasting perfumed ornaments that can be enclosed in mesh and hung with a ribbon in closets or tucked into drawers.

Journal about the positive mind benefits you experience after doing this activity.

Create a
Bucket List

The new moon opens itself to thought-provoking ideas. That's why it's a good time to create (or add to) your bucket list. Think about adventures you've yet to have; people you want to connect with; places you want to visit; something you want to purchase; a book you want to read; a movie you've always wanted to see; etc. Formulate and outline plans for how to accomplish one of these goals within the next month. Include what phase of the moon you think will be best for your activity.

Draw a Monthly Goal Tree

A goal tree is a fun tool to help structure and focus your mind around visualizing and achieving a personal goal. The trunk represents the core objective/purpose; the roots are the supporting values; and the branches and leaves are the primary and secondary actions. Follow these steps:

1. First, define your goal by asking: What do I want to do/to have/to learn? Then draw a picture of a tree. Write your goal on the trunk. Include a few critical determiners of your success so you'll have a clear idea of what the goal will look like when you reach it.

2. Note any supporting values and re-sources as roots.

3. Then add specific intermediate actions as branches and leaves; color them in when completed.

    With all the elements visually con-nected, this tool is sure to help you realize all your desires.

Time Travel in Your Mind

This exercise can help you figure out who you were in past lives and where you're going in the future. Follow these steps:

1. Imagine that you are at the entrance of a portal that can take you back in time or forward in time. The waxing moon will propel you to your destination. Write down where you find this portal (the desert, mountains, ocean, forest, your clothes closet, etc.). Is the portal a door, gate, or archway?

   _____

   _____

   _____

   _____

   _____

2. Think about where you want to go. Back or forward? Make a note of it. What do you want to achieve? Do you want to know who you were in a past life or who you are going to become in the future? Make the choice and write it down.

   _____

   _____

   _____

   _____

3. Get comfy. If you can get yourself in a meditative state, do it. If not, just concentrate on where you want to go. See yourself going through the portal and visualize what happens while you're at your destination.

4. Write about your experience when you come out of the portal. How do you feel and what did you discover?

   _____

   _____

   _____

   _____

   _____

   _____

   _____

   _____

   _____

   _____

   _____

   _____

   _____

   _____

   _____

   _____

   _____

Reflect On Your Experience with Karma

They say what goes around, comes around. Most of us have been wronged by someone else at some point in our lives, and many times we cope with these events by saying, "Karma will pay this person a visit eventually." On the other hand, we've all done things that we regret and that hurt others, whether intentionally or inadvertently. Believe it or not, someone out there has probably been hoping that karma catches up to you too! Can you think of a time or a situation where you felt like you were paying a cosmic price for something you did? How did that feel? What was the lesson in this?

Write Your Own Permission Slip

Many of us are overcommitted and trying to fit too much into our schedules. Too often, we find ourselves without enough time or energy to fully enjoy or meet our commitments. Besides, too many obligations create pressure and stress.

Taking a step back and sorting out which obligations are important and which aren't isn't always easy. Use this moon phase to give yourself permission to unburden yourself of at least one obligation. Ask yourself: What can I let go of? Not do or not attend? What duty can I delegate? If you're uncertain of which one, identify all your commitments, flag those that are nonnegotiable, then weed out anything that doesn't align with your values or doesn't nourish and energize you.

Select one and write out a consent form granting yourself permission to discard it. Then move on to incorporating more of what you *do* want in your life. That's when the growing frequency of the waxing moon will kick in. You just let go; now you build.

PERMISSION SLIP

Brainstorm Three Ways to Go Green

As the moon shifts from waxing to full, go with the moon flow and find ways to be more green. A more sustainable, eco-friendly world would have us all living a more mindful, slower, and more locally based and connected life. It requires shifting from a consumer-driven model to a conservator or stewardship economic model. Stewardship is taking care of something, such as making wise use of your thinking, time, and the natural and energy resources provided by the earth so that you might preserve life for future generations of Earth's inhabitants. For this activity, identify, list, and resolve to enact three new ways in which you can make this change and live a greener lifestyle. Examples of some possible changes include:

- Minimize water waste.

- Cut back on energy use in your home.

- Start a compost pile.

- Use paper less and recycle more.

- Use canvas bags instead of plastic.

- Borrow/share instead of buy.

1.

2.

3.

Track Your Full Moon Mood

The vibrational energy of the full moon affects everyone in different ways. Why not track your moods during full moons to see what it does to you? Check the circles that apply to you on this full moon. You'll do this exercise during each full moon to see if your mood stays the same or changes. *This full moon, I feel:*

○ Adventurous   ○ Healthy   ○ Magical

○ Anxious   ○ Hopeful   ○ Sexy

○ Athletic   ○ Intuitive   ○ So-So

○ Attractive   ○ In love   ○ Theatrical

○ Bored   ○ In lust   ○ Tired

○ Depressed   ○ Jealous   ○ Worried

○ Empowered   ○ Lonely   ○ _____

○ Generous   ○ Lost   ○ _____

Ask Yourself How You've Been

When the full moon is at her peak, Lady Luna can bring around people we haven't seen for a long time. That vibration has a way of calling on those who have been thinking about us to reach out. That said, even if you don't come across an old friend or someone you haven't been in touch with for a while, what would happen if you did see a long-lost buddy? Write down what you would say if they asked the question: What have you been doing lately? How would you respond? Would you tell them about your woes and sorrows? Would you lie and say everything is okay when it's not? Or would you tell them about all the positives that have happened? A mixture of everything? Be honest and pretend like that person is there in front of you and you have to answer immediately.

Draw Yourself As an Animal

Draw yourself as an animal you like that would describe who you are. The full moon will amplify that animal connection and make this process smoother. Next, draw a good friend as an animal. Why did you pick your animal? Why their animal? Example: Why are you a hawk and they are an eagle? Jot down a few characteristics of each animal that helps explain your choices.

Release Spiritual Blocks Using Lemon Balm Tea

Try a little ritual using lemon balm to get rid of spiritual blocks. First, though, write down what concerns you about your spiritual beliefs. Does it bother you that you were raised in a certain religion but now refer to yourself as nondenominational spiritual? Are you always searching for answers? Have you yet to find a meaningful spiritual connection? Relax, release, and give your higher power a chance to speak. The moon is waning, so release yourself from spiritual confusion.

You will need: lemon balm tea (which promotes spiritual growth), either loose or in a tea bag, and a small shallow container

1. Place the tea leaves in the container—or, if using a tea bag, tear it open and empty the leaves into the container. (You can even just place them in the palm of your hand.) Go outside to an open window or to a place that will allow you to blow the tea leaves away. Say, "I free confusion; mind unbound. Away it coasts; my spirit found."

2. Now blow the tea leaves away in any direction; they will find where they need to land.

3. Listen in the coming days for any incoming messages and write down what you experience.

Free Yourself from Mental Clutter

Modern humans are buried in unnecessary stuff. Some estimates say we've accumulated more clutter over the last hundred years than during the entire rest of human history! On top of material things, we're also drowning in mental clutter. After all, since the advent of digital technology, we're all inundated with more information than we know what to do with. All this data grabs our attention and eats up precious time and energy. This often leads to increased levels of stress. And boy, we have enough of that!

Just as we need to clean up our living spaces, our minds require decluttering so that we can focus on what is most important, is most meaningful, and brings us the greatest joy. Focused breathing, meditation, mindfulness, and the five-sense method can help keep you in the here and now and free your mind from overwhelming, debilitating thoughts and runaway feelings. Today, gaze at the waning moon for a few moments. Let its calm serenity wash over you before journaling about how you can simplify the mental clutter in your life.

Write to an Imaginary Friend, Angel, or Friendly Being

Do you believe in the existence of angels? What about extraterrestrial beings? Do you believe that people who have died are still in touch in some way? Not all of your friends have to be of this planet. The important thing is that they help and listen to you. Use the soothing light of the waning moon to bring these friendly beings front and center in your mind. There may be a lot more out there if you look and reach out.

   Write down what your cosmic friends look like and note what kind of personalities they have. Now write one of them a note sharing your feelings and expressing your gratitude for their friendship.

Dear   ,

Be a Shadow

A waning moon phase calls us to release. The October nights, with the hint of winter in the air, reminds us to be prepared for the near future. Combine the two; release your desires and get to know yourself a little better. Who would you want to be if you could be someone else and have their life? Think of someone you would like to be—it could be a celebrity, a friend, or a mentor. If you could shadow them for a day, what do you think it would be like? Start with getting out of bed in the morning. Do they get up early or late? Do they eat breakfast or not? Write down in detail how you think their day unravels. When you're done, circle or highlight what you liked and cross out what you don't like. See if you can incorporate any aspects you liked that can make you feel more like yourself. Celebrate who you are, now and always.

November

Focus On Gratitude

Trees once leafy green and later decked out in all of autumn's glorious colors are now barren. Fields are bare. The earth is immersed in ever-increasing darkness. It's time to count your blessings, give thanks, and recognize your place in the food chain and the cycle of life and death.

Be mindful and kind. Spend time thinking about where and how food comes to your table; express gratitude to and acknowledge the hard work of farmers and ranchers, along with the many people who produce and provision the food that nourishes and sustains you and your loved ones.

Be aware of and generous with those less fortunate and without many resources. Give what you can to those in need. Any act of kindness, no matter how small, echoes throughout the lives of those with whom we share. Bigheartedly donate money, food, clothing, household goods, and opportunities for work. Remember the animals; set out bird seed for birds that overwinter in your area.

Take special care of your health as colder weather settles in. Be sure to eat properly, bolstering your immune system with teas, herbs, and supplements to fortify you through the annual cold and flu season.

List Eight
Items You Love

It's easy to forget how fortunate we are. Thankfully, the essence of the new moon triggers a time of gratitude as it continues to appear in the night sky. It's time to echo that phase of growing light by thinking of people, places, and things that have made you happy. The act of writing down what you love will bring those things to the front of your mind and help them stay there.

Make a list of things you already have that you love. Is it that pink cat stuffed animal you've had since childhood or those new shoes you spent your paycheck on? Might it be your partner, who cooks delicious meals? Your dog? Try to list at least eight items and reflect on them. Where did they come from? Did you have to save to buy them, or were they a gift from nature, like that special seashell you found on the beach?

1.

2.

3.

4.

5.

6.

7.

8.

Take Your Goals Up a Notch

Go back to the goals you made in January. Now is the moment to go one step further, when the new moon beckons you to start to think about thriving. This lunar phase will help you enhance your goal setting. Use this quote by screenwriter, actress, and producer Lena Waithe as an inspiration: "Don't ask if your dream is crazy, ask if it's crazy enough." Have you achieved that business goal yet, or are you savoring a more casual plan? Walk to the beat of that different drummer within you and take it one step further. What changes can you make? If you have not reached your aspiration to this point, is there anything you should change?

_____

_____

_____

_____

_____

_____

_____

_____

_____

_____

_____

_____

_____

_____

Volunteer Your Time

The November winds reminds us that warmth and comfort are not only important to us, but also to others. Choose a way to volunteer for an organization or even assist just one person who needs support. You can have in-person encounters—for example, if you are a musician, volunteer to play at a local nursing home that may not have some of the funds the more elaborate facilities have. Help friends in need who may be too proud to ask for help; ask them if they could take the extra milk or vegetables off your hands, as you bought too much. Use your artistic skills to teach crafts to children at a local recreation center or library. Alternatively, you could share skills that allow you to stay home but make a difference, such as designing websites or flyers or sending out emails. The new moon sheds little light, but you too will sparkle when you give to others and are grateful you had the opportunity to help. Take pleasure in the soothing reward of giving.

Appreciate the Small Steps You Take

Keep your eye on the prize! As they say, "Inch by inch, life's a cinch, and mile by mile, life's a trial." So inch it, if you have to. If you are dieting and lose one pound, that's an accomplishment. Be proud you didn't gain or stay the same! The moon doesn't change phases overnight; she takes her time and builds momentum. You can operate the same way! Document any little accomplishments you've made that will eventually take you to your goals.

Give Yourself a Trophy

It may have been a while since you've gotten a trophy. Let's end that drought now. Draw yourself a trophy, and write on it something you've done recently that made you feel you deserve it. For example: helped a friend, wrote a chapter, did the laundry, got through a holiday without arguing with a family member, etc. Nothing is too small to celebrate. Give yourself a pat on the back and keep up the good work. It's spiritual growth in the making. This moon phase acts as a reminder that you can grow and be grateful for your success. When you're done, you may want to make a trophy for someone else to share the good feelings.

Challenge Yourself to Smile

Whether you are male or female, looks aren't everything…but confidence is important. Try taking what I call the smile challenge. It's amazing what a smile can do for your inner well-being. Do an experiment. Take a day and smile more than normal (not like a fool, of course; within reason). Smiles make others feel encouraged that happy people are all around, regardless of what they look like or are doing. Maybe that essence of bliss will transfer over to you. It's important to be around positive people when we can. Like the waxing moon keeps expanding its glow, you should expand your inner glow. When you come home at the end of the day, jot down how it made you feel, and how other people reacted to you. I tried this recently and it made me feel really good. The waxing moon time is always fun as it enhances things—all the more reason to smile!

Relive a Beautiful Childhood Memory

Enter a magnificent memory from child-hood you will never forget. Even if you don't have too many spectacular recollec-tions, there is always one that can be found and cherished. Think back to the senses you engaged during the moment—smells, tastes, sounds, etc.—as well as the logistics of the situation. When did this take place, how old were you, who were you with? Try to put words to paper to bring the image back to life. What kind of feeling did it give you? What emotions did you have? Write down why it was such a beautiful memory. The moon repeats her phases every month; could you repeat this mem-ory, or was it a one-time thing that you'd rather leave as it is?

Track Your Full Moon Mood

The vibrational energy of the full moon affects everyone in different ways. Why not track your moods during full moons to see what it does to you? Check the circles that apply to you on this full moon. You'll do this exercise during each full moon to see if your mood stays the same or changes. *This full moon, I feel:*

<table>
<tr><td>○ Adventurous</td><td>○ Healthy</td><td>○ Magical</td></tr>
<tr><td>○ Anxious</td><td>○ Hopeful</td><td>○ Sexy</td></tr>
<tr><td>○ Athletic</td><td>○ Intuitive</td><td>○ So-So</td></tr>
<tr><td>○ Attractive</td><td>○ In love</td><td>○ Theatrical</td></tr>
<tr><td>○ Bored</td><td>○ In lust</td><td>○ Tired</td></tr>
<tr><td>○ Depressed</td><td>○ Jealous</td><td>○ Worried</td></tr>
<tr><td>○ Empowered</td><td>○ Lonely</td><td>○ _____</td></tr>
<tr><td>○ Generous</td><td>○ Lost</td><td>○ _____</td></tr>
</table>

_____

_____

_____

_____

_____

_____

_____

_____

_____

_____

_____

List People Who Changed Your Life

Make a list of people—alive, dead, strangers, songwriters, writers, musicians, chefs, teachers, etc.—who have changed your life for the better, whether they know it or not. If you can't remember their names, no worries. For example, *the friendly person at the gas station* is good enough to write down. You will be surprised at how sometimes the smallest things people do make the biggest difference in your life. When you practice gratitude, you are happy, and when you are happy, your vibration lifts and more good comes your way. Positive vibes accumulate like the full moon has accumulated all the light she can hold and now showers that light upon you.

Record Your
Best Spells

Have you ever tried a spell or ritual, and then it worked better than you ever thought it would? It's hard to keep track of all the spells you try, so start documenting your successes. Write down as many details as you can think of about your best spells: the weather, your mood, who was in the house, and so forth. Even if it happened long ago, bring that memory back just like this full moon has made its cycle and come back. If you find yourself remembering a spell that didn't work, consider trying it again with slight changes.

Get Rid of Envy

We all encounter envy at one time or another, but this exercise will help you turn that negative energy into positive. Make a list of things someone else has that you want *and* why you are happy for them. The moon appears to diminish in the sky every month, and so should envy. By focusing on a reason you're happy for the person, you can savor and share their joyful energy instead of focusing on what you don't have. Turn envy into gratitude, and life flows so much better.

Person's Name	What They Have That You Want	Why You're Happy for Them

It is no secret that the moon has no light of her own, but is, as it were, a mirror, receiving brightness from the influence of the sun.

—Vitruvius, architect

Empty Your "Cauldron" of Goals That Aren't Working

Okay, it doesn't have to be a real cauldron. We all need to make time to "pour out" ideas that aren't working in our lives. Do you want to be a professional singer, but you have the voice of a moose who cut his hoof? You love to paint, but your abstracts give people headaches? You should certainly believe in yourself, but it's also good to consider that maybe the universe has something else in mind for you. The waning moon is a great time to cut your losses or at least put them on the back burner.

You will need: a vessel and some water

1. To ritualize this sentiment of letting go, fill a vessel of some type with water.

2. Look into the water and visualize your idea that is not working. Give it a blessing, such as, "May this idea flow back into the universe and be connected to the right person."

3. Pour the water down the sink while saying these words:

   "I walk in wonder, sun, or thunder, open to a different way.

   Fill my path with stones of insight. So it is and so I say."

You have just created a void like the waning moon inspires us to do. Now you can fill it, so think about what you can create when the moon starts to wax.

List Your Special Talents

Get rid of any lack of confidence you feel, just like the waning moon slowly removes her light. We all have special talents, but we rarely stop to appreciate what they are. I have even heard people say, "I'm just not good at anything!" That is not true at all. You just haven't thought hard enough. Write down gifts you have that you are grateful for. Here are some suggestions to get you started:

- ○ Personality
- ○ Patience
- ○ Making people laugh
- ○ Dealing with animals
- ○ Working with your hands
- ○ Intuition
- ○ Kindness
- ○
- ○
- ○
- ○
- ○
- ○
- ○
- ○

Contemplate Your Relationship with Tough Love

Tough love is difficult to define, but it's more or less when we force someone else to face or take responsibility for their actions. Has anyone ever given you a shot of tough love? Who was it, and how did it help you? Or did it? Tell your story. Put down the details—the who, what, where, and why. How did you come out of the situation? Confident, exhausted, self-reliant? Is there any way to see that tough love as a gift now?

Try filling in this sentence to see the silver lining:

The best thing that _____

ever did was to _____

_____

_____ .

Because of this, I am now_____

_____

_____ .

Have you ever helped someone else with the same method?

December

Release Negative Emotions

Blanketed with snow...silent and watched over by a vigilant, hopeful moon...much of the earth is sleeping now, resting, dreaming, and rejuvenating. As we move closer to the winter solstice, the nights grow longer and the darkness deepens, creating a magical and mysterious world full of wonder and peace. Celebrate the rebirth of the sun and remember far more is going on now than meets the eye. Once a new year is born, the days start to lengthen, light grows, and the cycle of renaissance and all that it promises begins again.

Now is the perfect time to cuddle up with a warm blanket by the fire and stay near to family, home, and hearth. Get plenty of sleep; recharge; reflect; clear the slate; and renew. Look back at the old year and review what you experienced, applaud your strengths, and admire your accomplishments. Confront any darkness you find within; banish grudges; forgive your own and others' sins; and unburden yourself of any negativity. This is an excellent time to work with dream magic—start a dream journal, learn to interpret your dreams, and leverage the inner inspiration.

Contemplate the Winter Season

As the new moon arrives this wintery month, consider what winter means to you. Draw a picture that resonates with winter to you. You can illustrate a tree (found in any region) that represents this season. If you live in a cool or cold climate, you may have marveled at snowflakes in all shapes and sizes falling down like magic. If you live in a tropical climate, sometimes the temperature dropping to 50°F is a wintry feeling to behold! Compare your thoughts about winter to those about the other seasons.

Identify an Area for Improvement

The new moon is whispering, "It's time for thinking, cultivating, and educating." Think of your life and what you could do to improve on it. Divide your day (let's say yesterday) into three categories: morning, afternoon, and evening. Journal what you did and how you would change anything. Would you have gotten up ten minutes earlier so you didn't have to rush so much in the morning? Would you have gone outside for a walk at lunchtime to enjoy some fresh air? Would you have shut off your devices earlier and slept more last night? Write whatever occurs to you and try to slowly implement some of your ideas.

Morning:

_____

_____

_____

_____

_____

Afternoon:

_____

_____

_____

_____

_____

Evening:

_____

_____

_____

_____

_____

_____

Have Your Traced Hand Read

Long-distance healing and psychic readings are quite common. Healers and readers are working with energy, and they can assess that in many different ways, so it's actually very possible to do this type of work from afar. For example, some people send hand tracings to readers (or *clairsentients*, meaning "clear feeling"—someone who can read energy intuitively) via snail mail. The reader or healer will feel the paper you drew on and pick up your vibrations, and can convey messages about your energy.

To make a simple hand tracing (like kids do), trace your hands next to each other on a separate piece of paper. After you trace, hold your hand there for a few moments to imprint some of your energy onto the paper. You can even dip your hand in a mixture of nontoxic blue (the color of healing) food coloring and water, and then make the imprint and drawing. There is really no wrong way to trace when energy is concerned. Send the original copy to the reader or healer, and see what they have to say! Respond to their notes here.

Appreciate a Good Cry

Crying does not mean you are weak—on the contrary, letting the tears flow is often the shortest and bravest path to overcoming whatever situation is plaguing you at the moment. As you come into the full power of the moon, think about the last time you had a good cry. Jot down notes about the experience. What event led to your tears? How did you feel before you cried, and how did you feel afterward? Think about a crying spell as a way to reclaim your power by releasing the sadness, fear, anger—whatever it is. Dry those eyes, wash your face, and look into the mirror—that's the face of a warrior!

Identify Helpful Coping Skills

As the moon's light becomes more visible, our emotions can get revved up. This isn't a bad thing, but it does help to be aware of how you're feeling and to have a plan to deal with intense emotions during this time. Happiness and positive energy are easy—no need to worry about those! But what are the best ways for you to calm fear, anger, anxiety, or sadness? Think about some of these coping skills and add your own soothing activities to this list. Refer to it as needed.

O   Listening to music

O   Journaling

O   Coloring or drawing

O   Meditating

O   Exercising (walking can be a huge help!)

O   Talking with a trusted friend

O   Making a cup of chamomile tea

O   Taking a soothing detoxifying bath

O

O

O

O

Make Three Winter Wishes

We know the waxing moon is about multiplication and abundance, so let's make three special winter wishes. Write down your three wishes here. Keep them simple—ten words or fewer for each wish. Don't cheat by adding *and*. For example, *I will get that job and move across the country* is two wishes, not one. This moon phase does have a way of making us insatiable, but the universe knows!

Once you've written the wishes, put an arrow pointing up next to each wish. As you draw the arrow, see that wish doing a liftoff into the ether. Next month, write down the results in the next waxing moon section.

1.
_____
_____

2.
_____
_____

3.
_____
_____

Track Your Full Moon Mood

The vibrational energy of the full moon affects everyone in different ways. Why not track your moods during full moons to see what it does to you? Check the circles that apply to you on this full moon. You'll do this exercise during each full moon to see if your mood stays the same or changes. *This full moon, I feel:*

○ Adventurous	○ Healthy	○ Magical
○ Anxious	○ Hopeful	○ Sexy
○ Athletic	○ Intuitive	○ So-So
○ Attractive	○ In love	○ Theatrical
○ Bored	○ In lust	○ Tired
○ Depressed	○ Jealous	○ Worried
○ Empowered	○ Lonely	_____
○ Generous	○ Lost	_____

De-stress with a Ritual Bath

When the moon is shining its brightest, you may be thinking about a well-deserved break. Those holiday events and obligations can quickly transform from high energy to exhaustion. Don't wait till the moon's light is vanishing for relaxation. Treat yourself to a full moon ritual bath. Utilize the light, energy, and magical time of year to relax.

First, let's make a little rosemary water (well known as "the herb of joy") to use in your bath. This will calm you down and restore your balance. Here's how to set up your bath.

You will need: fresh or dried rosemary and a pot of water

1. Boil the water and submerge your fresh or dried rosemary.

2. Let the water simmer and pour the rosemary water into your full bathtub. Let your imagination run for a couple of moments on things you want to do for the coming year.

3. Then let yourself just be, relax, and not even think at all. Just sit, soak, and get serene.

Turning the momentum of the full moon on its head may be just what you need at this time of year.

*The sky was a midnight-blue,
like warm, deep, blue water,
and the moon seemed to
lie on it like a water-lily,
floating forward
with an invisible current.*

—Willa Cather, author, One of Ours

Meditate On Your Health

The moon is winding down and so should you. Instead of being active, sit in any meditative position that suits you. Be comfortable. Set up all those comfort enhancements (music, candlelight, and so on) that put you into an altered state of consciousness. Now close your eyes and see your body in any way you choose to visualize it. Picture a healthy, happy you. What are you eating? How do you feel? What are you doing? What are you wearing? Write or draw what you visualized so you can refer back to it.

Breathe Out Those Negative Vibes

The quickest way to release stuck energy can sometimes be the best. The moon is waning, so blow out your stuck emotions and get rid of them. Lady Luna is doing it, so why not you? Before bed, sit for a moment and think of things in your life you want to discharge and write them down here.

Then inhale and blow out through your mouth, making a sound like blowing a whistle. Visualize gray smoke coming out of your mouth to represent the negative frequency you may be connected to. Do this three times. It's very freeing!

Write a Letter and Burn It

The end of the year is a good time to let go of an event or situation that's bothering you. In this exercise, you'll take something out of your head, put it on paper, and then destroy it. It's a physical representation of getting it out of your life for good.

    Write a letter to someone who has hurt you, describing what happened and the effect it had on your life. It may be a lingering pain from childhood, or it may be an event that's more recent. Write a really meaningful letter packed with emotion. Whether the person is still in your life anymore or not, don't let them take your joy. When you're done, carefully burn the letter in a fireplace or fireproof vessel as you say, "My past is gone, and I stay strong." Take a deep breath and move on!

◖ Let Go of a Past Friendship

We all would love to keep friends forever, but sometimes people come into our lives to teach us something and then they go along their way. Reflecting on this sentiment is especially useful in the month of December, when we are recalling events from the past year. Did you find yourself struggling to connect with a friend? Maybe you now have different lifestyles or interests than you did when you met and became friends. It might be time to let this friendship go. The waning moon makes it easier, as it's cheering for us to make this situation smaller and smaller and smaller. Write a short story about friendship with a joyful ending that shows how the friends came into each other's life for a purpose, and then went their separate ways. Thank the universe for looking out for you and your friends, current or former.

Reflect On the Year

The year is coming to an end, and the moon is waning as well. Take some time now to reflect on the past year. Write down your triumphs and tribulations, your successes and your failures. Add what you're glad to leave behind and what you're most looking forward to.

In the future (a few months from now, or even next December), look back at this page and see how you feel about what you wrote, especially anything negative. Is that event you saw as a failure now the best thing that ever happened to you? Was that event you were excited about actually dreadful? The moon is removing its light and transitioning, so you should too, by removing thoughts of defeat or disappointment. Let your light shine!

INDEX

Tap In to the Hidden Power of the Moon!

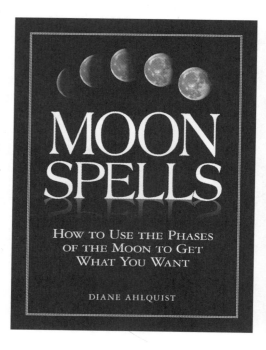